# SIX DEGREES OF EDUCATION

Ignatius Chithelen was a reporter for *Forbes* and has written for *Barron's, Knowledge@Wharton and The New York Times*. His six degrees include journalism from Columbia University, philosophy and political science from Mumbai University and economics from the Centre For Development Studies, India. A fund manager, and a Chartered Financial Analyst, he is based in New York.

Bryant Park Publishers

# SIX DEGREES OF EDUCATION

From Teaching in Mumbai to Investment Research in New York

IGNATIUS CHITHELEN

BRYANT PARK PUBLISHERS

Copyright © 2016 by Ignatius Chithelen

All rights reserved. Thank you for your support of the author's rights.
In accordance with the U.S. Copyright Act of 1976, the scanning, uploading, and electronic sharing of any part of this book without the permission of the publisher constitute unlawful piracy and theft of the author's intellectual property. If you would like to use material from the book (other than for review purposes), prior written permission must be obtained by contacting the publisher at contact@bryantparkpublishers.com.

Published by Bryant Park Publishers LLC
New York

www.bryantparkpublishers.com

Published in the United States

Library of Congress Cataloging-in-Publications Data:
Names: Chithelen, Ignatius
Title: Six Degrees of Education: From Teaching in Mumbai to Investment Research in New York/ Ignatius Chithelen
Description: First Edition./ New York: Bryant Park Publishers, 2016.
Identifiers: Library of Congress Cataloging Number: 2016905484
ISBN: Hardback: 978-0-9974703-2-1
ISBN: e-book: 978-0-9974703-1-4
ISBN: Paperback: 978-0-9974703-0-7
ISBN: e-pub: 978-0-9974703-3-8
ISBN: MOBI: 978-0-9974703-4-5
Subjects: Non-fiction – Education, journalism and investment research/India-Education/India-Politics/India-Economics
BISAC: BIOGRAPHY & AUTOBIOGRAPHY/Personal Memoirs./EDUCATION/Students & Student Life. BUSINESS/Investments & Securities-stocks.

Cover design by: Visakh Menon

Typeface: Minion, produced by Adobe Corp; designed by Robert Slimbach
Manufactured in the United States of America
First United States Edition

For my children Anna, Natalie and Niall: perhaps you will find some answers and more questions.

"If he laughs well, he is a good man."
Fyodor Dostoevsky

# CONTENTS

|     | Preface: A Goat, not an Asian Tiger | 11 |
| --- | --- | --- |
| 1 | Cure for Writer's Block | 16 |
| 2 | Eleven Years of School for $120 | 40 |
| 3 | Losing Santa Claus in Mumbai | 50 |
| 4 | Reach for the Sky | 60 |
| 5 | An Accident Finishing High School? | 67 |
| 6 | Close, but no Medical Studies | 78 |
| 7 | A Teacher Nicknamed Charlie Chaplin | 89 |
| 8 | Gray Hair During Indira Gandhi's Emergency | 103 |
| 9 | Five Religions, Four Castes & 22 Languages | 114 |
| 10 | The Power of Sugar Barons | 131 |
| 11 | Hindu-Muslim Violence for Political Gains | 153 |
| 12 | A Tiny Widget in a Capitalist Tool | 166 |
| 13 | An Investment Analyst on Wall Street | 176 |
| 14 | Funding Free Classic Books | 191 |
|     | Appendix A: *The Economist* Thrives | 194 |
|     | Appendix B: Disrupting For-Profit Academic Publishing | 199 |
|     | Appendix C: Indian Entrepreneurs in the U.S. | 203 |
|     | Acknowledgements | 207 |

## PREFACE: A GOAT, NOT AN ASIAN TIGER

In matters of education and careers, there is much discussion about Asian Tiger parents pressuring their kids to excel in math, science and music so they can get into Ivy League colleges and then work on Wall Street or as a plastic surgeon. In my case, while Indian, and hence Asian, I do not measure up to being a tiger. Perhaps I resemble a goat, my favorite animal as a kid, and because I am stubborn.

I made mistakes and switched careers several times: first in Mumbai from studying chemistry and teaching middle school to working for a weekly magazine. Then in New York, I went from a freelance writer to investment research. Fortunately I was shielded from the worst consequences of my errors by pursuing six degrees, or five and three quarter degrees to be precise.

My whole college career may have been an accident. I was hoping to join a merchant navy officer program in Mumbai after finishing 10$^{th}$ grade. I passed the competitive entrance exam for admission to a medical school but failed to qualify due to a low grade in the university final exam.

I switched to studying philosophy, after three of four years for a degree in chemistry; hence the ¾ degree. Then, by chance, I found the answers I sought from philosophy in the novels of Fyodor Dostoevsky.

I went on to get an MA in Political Science and an M.Phil. in Development Economics. I was 27 when I got my M.Phil., past the legal age limit for admission to all professional colleges, and for applying to good jobs for graduates in India. Four years later, in 1986, I graduated from the Columbia Journalism School in New York. In 1992, while working as a reporter at *Forbes,* I passed the third and final Chartered Financial Analysts exam, getting a sixth "degree." I then found a job as an investment analyst at SoGen (now First Eagle) Funds, run by the French bank Societe Generale, in New York.

All through my studies, I had teachers who encouraged curiosity, said there are no dumb questions and that it is good to reach for the sky. The majority of my teachers, especially in school, were mediocre. I also had some very bad teachers who, with one exception, were good people lacking teaching skills or interest in their jobs. The bad teacher in sixth-grade did not cause long-term harm perhaps because I had very good teachers in the fifth and seventh grades.

While discussing my education in India, I speak of the reliance on learning by rote; the high pressure one-shot essay based final exams; the continuing and expanding role of English based learning; the elite English language institutions and the poor quality of education delivered to the majority of students who study at government-funded institutions.

I look at the slim odds of getting into India's top medical, technology and management colleges, which are all government funded. The majority of Indian professionals working in the U.S. are graduates of these institutions. They are also more successful as entrepreneurs in the U.S. than professionals in India.

I jokingly tell those interested in India that it is a very easy country to understand: it has a large tribal population, twenty-two major languages, four castes, and five religions.

Despite such complexity, you can figure out the religion, the native language and, if Hindu, the caste from an Indian's first and last names. My names show I am a Christian from Kerala.

My master's degree in political science covered the alliances of caste, religious and linguistic groups that determine which political parties win state and central elections. I discuss why some politicians regularly incite violent conflicts, in which hundreds are killed, between Hindus and Muslims, between upper and lower caste Hindus, and between Hindus and Christians.

My M.Phil. studies gave me insights into how big farmers from the major castes, using their political and economic clout, control India's agricultural economy. Many argue that the bureaucratic hurdles faced by new entrants in business in India are due to the country's socialist legacy. Such barriers exist because they protect established businesses from new competitors and not due to any ideological overhang.

I learned that there is no such thing as writer's block while at the Columbia Journalism School in New York. I stumbled upon and got hooked on, value investing after reading a *Fortune* article on Warren Buffett. I then learned how to read financial statements while preparing for the CFA exams.

Investing, my current and longest career, is a strange twist since I had no desire to be rich. This personal conflict led to major problems after I set up my own fund.

In this recollection, besides good teachers, I talk about relatives and friends, including Sanjoy Ghose, a social worker in India; Charles Michener, a *Newsweek* editor who recommended me to the journalism school; and bosses Krishna Raj at the *Economic & Political Weekly* in Mumbai and Jean-Marie Eveillard at SoGen Funds in New York.

My description of them may be biased since they were good to me. From observing and speaking to them, I figured out ways to pursue my search for a career, learned to focus on my skills, rather than competing with others, and realized that it is OK to fail and to keep trying. Jean-Marie quotes Samuel Beckett "Ever tried. Ever failed. No matter. Try again. Fail again. Fail better."

I recall being a Catholic outsider in a Catholic school,

learning value investing from my grandmother by bargaining in Mumbai bazaars, fearing arrest during Prime Minister Indira Gandhi's 1975-77 dictatorship, avoiding physical assaults while in student politics, being saved after I nearly drowned, losing my briefcase with $3,880 raised in loans for the journalism school fees and learning about pricing, sales, profits, inventory and cash flow while selling at flea markets in New York.

I analyze the reasons for the continuing business success of *The Economist*, while other traditional magazine and newspaper publishers have been hit hard by the rise of digital media rivals. I also discuss how rivals, backed by academic associations and using digital technology, will likely disrupt the high margins enjoyed by for-profit academic publishers.

I am surrounded by teachers: daughter, mother, sister, brother, aunts, uncles, nieces, other relatives and lots of friends. I taught math and science in a middle school for three years and political science for a year at a college, both in Mumbai.

In India, where I went to school and college, everyone from parents to shopkeepers respect teachers. But they are paid poorly and, except in small towns and villages, they cannot support a family on their income. Most of my school teachers were women supplementing their husbands' income.

Various jobs and fellowships funded me for most of the fourteen years I spent getting college degrees. In India the total cost of my school and college education were actually negative. Overall I got more government cash funding - excluding subsidies - than the total tuition and other fees paid by my parents and me.

My job continues to be managing investments. I worked on this book on weekends, in part by giving up golf and squash, both of which I play badly. I do not know the rules of English grammar and so made revisions based on how I think a sentence should read. The book has taken me nearly five years to finish.

I owe a debt to give back, at the very least, the full market cost of the heavily subsidized education that I got in India and the grants for my journalism study in the U.S. I plan to do this by trying to expand access to informal education, through free distribution of major classic texts of knowledge. I also intend to help promote civil liberties.

My journey as a bumbling goat remains unfinished.

# Chapter 1

## CURE FOR WRITER'S BLOCK

"There is an easy cure for writer's block," Bob used to tell students in his magazine writing class at the Columbia Graduate School of Journalism in New York. "Just sit at a table and type or write down all the ideas that come to you on the topic, even if they seem vague and unrelated. Helpful if you can write a good lead sentence but OK if you cannot," he added.

"Expand on the ideas by adding facts and points of view," Bob said, "again writing down everything that comes to mind. Put in specific information, instead of general descriptions. This makes the piece tighter. Add lots of color and anecdotes to make it livelier. Then you organize the text logically, telling a story, discard stuff that does not strengthen the main point of view and write an introduction and conclusion."

Bob was Robert C. Christopher, an adjunct professor at the journalism school. He was also the Secretary of the Pulitzer Prize Board from 1981 till his passing in 1992 from emphysema at age 68. He was a former International Editor of *Newsweek* and earlier spent thirteen years at *Time*.

I was one of eight students who took his spring semester course at the school, in the Class of 1986. I chose the course because of Bob's career and since I liked writing analytical pieces, which are typically found in magazines. I had no interest in covering breaking news stories, a goal of many fellow students. I had also worked at the *Economic & Political Weekly* in Mumbai before enrolling at the school.

Like all good teachers, Bob enjoyed spirited arguments with his students. Once when the formulaic format of newsmagazine writing came up for discussion, Bob said the writing used to be much worse. He spoke about Wolcott Gibbs' satirical article in *The New Yorker* in November 1936, "Time...Fortune...Life...Luce."

The article included this imitation of *Time* style: "Backward ran sentences until reeled the mind." Though he spent decades writing for *Time* and *Newsweek*, Bob often said that the best writing was by Ernest Hemingway and in the St. James Bible.

Bob said with a grin that the reader he had in mind while writing for the newsweeklies was a Cincinnati dentist who was too busy to read the daily newspaper. His writing methods helped him and other writers and editors at American newsweeklies produce hundreds of pages of articles each week under tight deadlines, based on stories sent by reporters and researchers.

Perhaps this newsweekly writing process is the journalistic equivalent of the assembly line system to mass produce cars introduced by Henry Ford.

I find Bob's methods very helpful for my writing, including this work. The importance of disciplined writing each day, for a set number of hours, and not waiting for inspiration to strike, is a technique used by many notable writers of fiction and non-fiction.

After graduating from the school, I met Bob about once a semester at a Chinese restaurant he liked on the east side of Broadway between 110th and 111th Street. Over beer and $5.95 lunch specials, we would discuss major events, my work and goals, and his writing and book plans. He wrote three books, including *Crashing the Gates: the Dewasping of America's Power Elite*.

Bob discussed the illusory power of journalists during one of our lunches. He said that when he was an editor at *Newsweek* the most powerful politicians, businessmen and bureaucrats around the world would return his call in a few minutes. But after he left the weekly magazine, even those he thought were friends in high places would not return his calls.

Bob was over six feet tall and gangly, with gray hair and large glasses with thick lenses. His hands shook and he had a raspy voice from smoking. Proud of his Canadian White Anglo-Saxon ancestors, Bob told the story of often being mistaken for an Irish American at the Irish pubs in midtown Manhattan. Late at night, after several drinks, the other patrons would ask him when he was returning to Ireland.

In April 1987, Bob was a reference for the reporter's job I got at *Forbes*. Two years earlier, Charles Michener, Bob's former colleague at *Newsweek*, had recommended me to the Columbia journalism school.

## Leaving $3,880 in a New York Cab

During my early weeks at the Columbia Journalism School, many American fellow students asked if I experienced culture shock in New York since it was my first visit to the city and, in fact, my first travel outside India. I said I was shocked instead by the clumsy loss of my briefcase.

I arrived at John F. Kennedy Airport on Sunday September 1, 1985, after a 22-hour journey from Mumbai. From the airport I took a bus to Grand Central terminal holding my black leather briefcase in my hand. I then took a taxi to the apartment building in Greenwich Village where Indrani Rahman, mother of a friend Ram, lived and where I was to stay that night.

In the taxi I watched the fare on the meter, instead of the city around me, and got nervous when it rose beyond $4. This was higher than what Ram said was the typical cost for the thirty block ride. I wondered if the cabbie was driving to a place where he would mug me.

Ram and other Indians who had visited New York, warned me to be wary of muggers, including cab drivers. They advised I carry "mug money," at least $30 in cash. If mugged, I was told to quickly hand over the cash, my wallet and watch, without any arguments or hesitation, to avoid being shot by the mugger.

I was soon relieved to see the taxi had reached my building. Ram's mother was at work teaching a classical Indian dance class. After about twenty minutes of enjoying a warm water bath, I started thinking of people I should phone in New York. I panicked since I could not recall if I had my briefcase, which contained my address book.

I quickly got out of the tub, got dressed and looked around. No briefcase. It had $500 in cash, an American Express check for $3,380 and my passport. The money was raised in loans, mostly from Parsi foundations in Mumbai, to pay part of the roughly $22,000 in fees and expenses for the nine-month Masters' program at Columbia's Journalism School.

I could not recall where I had left the briefcase. I searched areas of the apartment I had not even visited. While looking inside a closet, I pulled the door so hard that a framed painting, hung on the wall, fell to the floor shattering its glass. I crawled and picked up the glass pieces with my bare hands and got cut.

Indrani was generous saying the broken glass was a sign of good luck. She took me out to dinner, but I do not remember what restaurant or what I ate for my first meal in America. That night I called a friend in Mumbai asking him to contact the local branch of American Express and cancel the lost check.

The next morning, Labor Day, I went to the 9th Police Precinct in Greenwich Village to report my lost briefcase. The cop was skeptical asking, "Are you sure it was not stolen from you?"

I then took my bag, got on the number 1 subway and went to 362 Riverside Drive at 110th Street, which was a residence for graduate students of Columbia University. After filling out a few forms, I was assigned to a suite with fourteen other students.

On Tuesday, skipping the inaugural lectures at the school, I went to the Indian consulate to apply for a new passport. I found out I had to get a police report about my lost passport before I could apply for a new one. So I returned to the 9th Police Precinct.

Around 4 p.m., after I got the police report and applied for a new passport, I went to the International Students Office at Columbia University to apply for a new U.S. visa. "Tired and disheartened," as I wrote in an article on this experience published in *New York Newsday*. "I sat on a sofa in the office, reflecting on the possible length of the ordeal and its likely outcome."

Lost in thought, I was startled when the young woman in the office asked if she could help me. I told her I would like to apply for a new visa since I had lost my passport. She asked my name and, since it is long and unusual, asked me to write it down.

She went into a back office and came back smiling and said, "You have a good angel looking after you. Somebody found your briefcase and called us." She then wrote down a name and a phone number and gave it to me.

I called David Platkin from a payphone in the building basement and went to his apartment on east 37th street. He said he found the briefcase in a cab and had tried various ways to contact me, including through the Indian consulate, since he did not want me to miss getting a degree from Columbia because I lost a large part of my funding.

I gave David the briefcase, after emptying the contents into another bag. I walked west to a Hudson River Pier on 42nd street with no thoughts of being mugged. On the waterfront, I joined my classmates for a Circle Line cruise around New York harbor, hosted by Osborn Elliott, the dean of the school.

A few weeks later, I typed a roughly 800-word article on my experience. I sent it to Amei Wallach a writer at *Newsday*. I had met her the previous summer in Mumbai through Zette Emmons, Ram's roommate in New York.

*New York Newsday* published the piece on November 15, 1985, under the title, "The Briefcase I Feared Was Stolen." I learnt of its publication that afternoon from a written note congratulating me from Pete Johnston, the J school academic dean, which I found in my mail box. *Newsday* paid me $75.

I was similarly lucky to have people return my lost wallet on three other occasions in the U.S., including after leaving it in a restroom at Chicago's busy, crowded O'Hare airport one summer evening. In September 2015, repeating my Chicago blunder, I left an envelope with $245 in cash in a restroom at the Grand Hyatt Hotel in New York while attending an investment conference. That time I did not get the money back.

I have found several wallets and cell phones and called the owners and returned the items to them personally. I was told by a cop whom I know that this is the best thing to do since expensive items and cash can disappear from a lost and found office.

### No Shaking Hands

Many journalists argue that you cannot teach good journalism. Some point to Great Britain where the craft has flourished for centuries without major journalism schools. Most good journalists, in addition to reporting, research and writing skills, have a grasp of the topics they cover either through advanced education, extensive reading or by talking to the right experts - and often a combination of all three.

The focus of the Columbia Journalism School in the mid-1980s was to prepare most of its class of 180 students for print newspaper and magazine jobs in the U.S. They were then thriving businesses, and most in my class found such jobs upon graduation.

Many of my fellow students had come to the school after working for a college or small newspaper in America. Only a few students took the major television and radio courses since there were few job openings.

The more ambitious students wanted to work for *The New York Times*, win a Pulitzer Prize, write bestselling books and get a story made into a hit Hollywood film. Today, with the rise of free online media decimating the print media business, only a handful of my classmates work as print journalists. Many of them work for non-profit groups.

To me, one of 15 foreign students, the school was appealing for three reasons. The MS program was only two semesters. After spending nearly eleven years for various degrees, I did not want to spend more time in academia.

Second, the course work emphasized on-the-job training. For instance, my first assignment for the Reporting and Writing course was to interview and write a story on the homeless men then living at the southern end of Madison Square Park at 23rd Street and Broadway.

Today, at the same corner of the park, there are long lines of people waiting to buy hamburgers, crinkle fries, hot dogs and milkshakes at the lawyer-turned-serial-restaurant-owner Danny Meyer's first Shake Shack outlet. The homeless are now to be found on the benches outside the park and at construction sites in various parts of the city, including on Fifth Avenue.

The third attraction of the J school was its location in New York City, the global center of the media business. Leading New York-based journalists taught as adjunct faculty, and the school invited a steady stream of leading print, TV and radio journalists to speak to students.

One of them was Andrew Knight, editor of *The Economist*. In November 1985, he delivered the annual lecture of the Bagehot Fellowship program, named after Walter Bagehot an editor of the weekly in the nineteenth century.

Knight also spoke to Beth Nissen's reporting and writing class. I was not in Nissen's class but attended his talk, since I was a regular reader of *The Economist* from around age eighteen.

Spending over an hour usually at libraries, I read it from cover to cover. Its concise, fact-based analytical pieces gave me weekly insights into the key political, economic, business and finance issues.

The weekly was founded in 1843 by a Scottish hat maker to champion free trade, internationalism and minimum interference by governments, especially in markets. (I discuss the attractive business of *The Economist* while rival legacy print publications are hit by free online news, in Appendix A.)

Under Knight, the circulation of the magazine had tripled in a decade to over 250,000. I asked him about the weekly's growth in U.S. circulation, then over 100,000, which was larger than that in the U.K.

After the class ended, I continued chatting with Knight as we walked down the stairs. When we parted, near the statue of Thomas Jefferson at the main entrance to the school building, perhaps displaying typical English aloofness, he did not give me his business card or even shake my hand.

Two months later, Knight was appointed Chief Executive and Editor in Chief of London based The Daily Telegraph Company. From 1990 to 1995, he was Executive Chairman of News International and then served on the board of directors of News Corporation, both controlled by Rupert Murdoch.

Knight was apparently one of the local managers who helped the Australian-born Murdoch outfox the long entrenched British elite to become a major owner of newspaper and TV properties in Britain. Through his media business, Murdoch continues to wield major influence over British politicians and policy. Knight studied at Ampleforth College, a Roman Catholic residential high school run by Benedictine monks in Yorkshire, and at Oxford University.

## British Lords and Dames

In the 1990s, I stopped reading *The Economist*, since I found very few fresh insights. This was largely because, as an investment analyst at SoGen Funds, each day I read *The Financial Times, The New York Times and The Wall Street Journal*. Also, possibly due to 40% of its circulation and likely more than half of its advertising and circulation revenues coming from the U.S., the weekly's coverage of the U.S. was less critical and incisive.

I mentioned this to Bill Emmott, editor of *The Economist*, following his talk at a club in New York in 2003. He animatedly said I was wrong to say the weekly's editorial policy was tilted towards the bias of most of its readers and advertisers from the U.S. I asked for his business card, so I could email him examples. He did not give me his card and, when we parted, he too did not shake my hand.

Maybe such attitudes are a continuation of the age old snobbery and class distinctions still practiced by the British elite. In the mid-1990s, at a conference in New York of major European companies, I was surprised to hear the finance chief of Sainsbury refer to his chief executive as "Sir Sainsbury." The executive of the major British retailer had been knighted by the Queen of England.

Marjorie Scardino, the American born former publisher of *The Economist*, was given a title by the Queen. She is referred to as Dame by British business publications including *The Financial Times*. She rose to become the Chief Executive of the Pearson Group, the parent of both the magazine and the newspaper.

In India, too, there are clear class distinctions on top of a caste hierarchy. The business and professional elite, especially alumni of the top private schools and colleges and executives of multinational corporations, rarely mix socially with those below them in the economic hierarchy. They inherited this custom from their former British rulers, though their Indian ancestors were snubbed by the British when they ruled the country.

Many Indian professionals in America, perhaps like other professionals, decide whether to socialize with a fellow Indian based on net worth, potential business and social networking value, as well as family status in India.

I have made more British friends in America than Indians, and more Chinese friends than British. The Chinese though, are from Hong Kong, which was a former British colony.

Such class hierarchy based customs are largely ignored in America, at least in most major cities, where money, skills and college define your social status. There is also more respect for lower level employees since many Americans have parents or grandparents who were poor or illiterate.

Yet, as many classic novels have covered, social climbing is a common human desire. Several Americans who are not white Protestants, especially the wealthy and professionals, eagerly seek to marry partners who are White Anglo-Saxon Protestants. They raise their children as Episcopalians and Presbyterians following such marriages.

This desire to become American Brahmans, including among politicians and their children, is seen in the upper crust claims in the weddings and fundraising events listed in the Style Section of *The New York Times*. The same politicians, however, loudly claim to come from humble origins, by speaking of their hardworking blue collar parents and grandparents when they are campaigning for elections.

Also, the deep racial tensions and divide continue, and the opportunities for good education and jobs remain few for the majority of the U.S. population.

## Spies at the United Nations

I had to rewrite several stories in the Reporting and Writing course, the core of the first semester classes at the journalism school. Dick Oliver, a reporter for *The Daily News* and adjunct teacher, would tell us to write as if we were in a bar telling the story to a friend or colleague. I tried, but my writing, showing the weight of my academic work, was not chatty and colorful.

The only story I wrote which Oliver liked was about Prime Minister Rajiv Gandhi's speech, at the School of International and Public Affairs in September 1985, on the prospects for India. In fact, he liked more the story of how I got to cover the story.

Ashok Mahadevan, editor of the *Reader's Digest India*, was in the press team accompanying the Prime Minister on his visit to the U.S. A journalism school alumnus, Ashok asked me to join him at the SIPA event. I showed my Columbia ID card and walked into the auditorium with him.

A few minutes later, a U.S. secret service agent asked me to step out saying he needed to check my ID. He checked my Columbia ID in the lobby but would not let me go back in. When I protested, he said he would let me in if I allowed him to search me. He frisked me in a restroom and let me go back in, but warning that he would deny frisking a Columbia student if I wrote a story about it. Such tight security measures were necessary because Rajiv Gandhi faced death threats. In 1991, he was assassinated by a bomb explosion in South India.

I took a course on reporting from the United Nations, taught by Kathleen Teltsch, the UN correspondent for *The New York Times*. She told lots of stories about scandals and the spies operating at the UN, many on journalist visas.

Charles Michener had told me about spies from the Soviet Union at the International House, when he stayed there while at the school of journalism. I applied to the house, but did not get in.

As for spies, it appears that a student in my UN class may have been trying to recruit foreigners for some U.S. agency. At his suggestion, we met and had our sandwiches in the park along the East River in the UN complex.

As we walked, he said his sister was a senior U.S. official and that her department was seeking foreign journalists to write for them for a good fee. I said nothing and quickly ended our walk, and he never mentioned it again.

Matt Cain, a student in the UN class, was in a two-year Master's joint degree program in journalism and international affairs. He was a regular reader of *The Economist* and challenged everything I said about the political, economic and social situation in India.

I had to write stories on political and economic topics for the UN course and so I did OK with them. Having grown up in India, I had the impression of the UN being a major force in global affairs since Indian newspapers extensively covered its events, actions and agencies. During Kathleen's class I found the UN to be largely a debating society, unless the U.S., Russia and other major powers all agreed to take some action.

I tried to find freelance or part-time work at the UN and its agencies. I only got a 20-hour job of condensing documents for an appendix to a report, thanks to Gerson da Cunha, a senior UNICEF official whose journalist wife Uma I knew from Mumbai.

The UN was worse in bureaucratic ways than the operation of government offices in India. I wrote and called several UN officials, many of them Indians, after meeting them at events or following an introduction. But their secretaries said they were in meetings and nobody called back. The officials likely ignored me since I had no ministers and senior officials to recommend me.

The UN class was held at the very formal UN headquarters near midtown east. I wore a suit to class that was stitched by a tailor in Mumbai's Fort area recommended by Mehlli Gobhai, an Indian artist, who lived in New York and Mumbai.

The suit was gray, a neutral color that I was told I could wear both day and night. I also got a couple of khaki trousers since it was what men in journalism and the arts wore in New York during the summer. In Mumbai khaki is the uniform for bus drivers and industrial workers.

The UN course was my second choice after International Reporting, for which I was not selected. Donald Shanor, who taught the international course, was the faculty member in charge of foreign students. He was tall, had a trim beard and wore a tie and tweed jackets. He met with the foreign students once a month to ask how we were faring. He also invited the students to a dinner at his apartment near Columbia.

## A Don McLean Concert at Carnegie Hall

My loans and grants covered only three quarters of the total cost of the journalism program. So I searched for jobs to fund the gap. The only job I got was at Columbia University's dining services, paying about $4 per hour plus two free meals, since few American students wanted such low wage physical jobs. I got a Social Security card for this jobs, through the university so that I could work as a foreign student.

I worked in the dining room on weekends. But I could do the job for only four weeks. My mind became numb after five hours of repetitive physical tasks, like serving food or cleaning tables. I am reminded of this experience when I go to a Starbucks store, since many of the staff look like students or recent graduates.

I found work at New York based *India Abroad*, about twenty hours a week including a full day on Saturday. The weekly tabloid summarized major news from India and covered news about Indians in the U.S. and Canada.

The India Abroad Foundation, run by Gopal Raju, the paper's publisher, gave a $5,500 fellowship to cover my fees for a semester at the journalism school. The dean of students, Monica Miya, helped me get the grant. She often asked how I was doing and offered advice, including on finding apartment shares.

*India Abroad* paid me five dollars an hour. I read and rewrote stories from Reuters and Associated Press news feeds. When I mentioned this wage to an Indian businessman, he said my effective hourly wage was much higher if the foundation's fellowship to the school was included.

During my first weeks in New York I often ate at Indian restaurants since Matt Cain, David Goldberg, Annette Kondo, Doug Wilson and a few other American classmates said they liked the food. Mostly we went to the "Indian" row on East 6th street between First and Second Avenues. I tried different restaurants there but found the same bland Bangladeshi food and at one place angrily asked if they all shared a common kitchen.

I later read in a *New York Times* article that the restaurants were owned by the brothers, uncles, cousins and other relatives of an immigrant from Sylhet, Bangladesh, who started the first one.

The food was cheap, roughly $5 per head, competing for the low end with Chinese food and Greek diners. Patrons could also bring their own beer and wine making the overall meal even cheaper. The Bangladeshi row deserves credit for popularizing Indian food in New York, which now has numerous Indian restaurants including several upscale ones.

For my regular meals I ate milk and cereals, bread, cheese

and bologna sandwiches, and 99 cents Whoppers from Burger King. I did this to save money, since I converted all expenses into Indian rupees and found everything very expensive.

In October, I had a severe stomach virus, which was only cured after two rounds of heavy medication. It is likely, as some friends from Mumbai pointed out, that I caught the virus in Mumbai and it got worse after I ate some stale bologna. Since then I can't eat spicy food, including most Indian dishes, and bologna.

David and I discussed a range of topics: the courses and teachers at the school, prospects for journalism careers, the Soviet Union, which he had visited, Fyodor Dostoevsky, American politics and music.

Just before Thanksgiving, David and I attended a concert by Don McLean at Carnegie Hall. While McLean was not a must-see musician, I was eager to see a live concert by a major artist. The concert brought back memories, as music often does, of my listening to a cassette of Don McLean songs at Navroz Seervai's parents' apartment in Mumbai.

David invited me to visit his family in Macon, Georgia, during the Christmas break. I was glad to get away from school and work and so was content staying in his house or going to the local library. David's friends would just show up to chat or to go to a movie or a bar, without calling in advance, similar to what we did as teenagers in Mumbai.

### Grab a Reader's Attention

During the second semester, I took a course in radio reporting, despite being shy about public speaking. The teacher Tom Phillips and an assistant Jane deserved their high reputation among students. They taped reports from students covering various events in the city and put it together as a broadcast. Since each report was only a couple of minutes long, we had to quickly condense the information into a few colorful sentences.

I took another minor course on film criticism. It was taught by Andrew Sarris, the film critic of *The Village Voice*, in a class with over two hundred students. An Israeli roommate from the engineering school recommended the class saying, "you get to watch a film every week and only have to write a brief film review." I wrote a review of "The Graduate," mostly repeating Sarris' point of view, and got a C.

I could not come up with a better topic for my Master's thesis and so chose to expand on my experience of finding my lost briefcase with the title "Fear of Crime in New York." I interviewed some New Yorkers who had been mugged and some experts on the topic. But, given the wide scope of the topic and the short time, my thesis was very superficial. The only remarkable thing about it was that I had to type the final draft twice.

Few students could afford to own computers in 1985, and so the school had a laboratory with about 20 computers where many students typed their papers. I had finished my thesis of about 3,000 words well before the deadline.

After revising it one last time, a blank screen showed up when I tried to save my work to a floppy disk. Prompted to save, I pressed enter. Then, when I tried to retrieve the file to print it, the file did not exist.

I spent much of the evening and night rewriting the thesis from rough drafts and missed the 5:00 pm deadline. Other students had similarly lost their saved files, and so my thesis adviser Joyce Shelby - and the school - were OK with my being a day late.

All the teachers at the journalism school, notably the dean,

Osborn Elliott, a former editor of *Newsweek*, emphasized writing stories with catchy opening sentences, lots of color and quotes and provocative last sentences, to attract a reader's attention.

Initially I ignored these suggestions assuming they were marketing gimmicks. But my opinion, I later realized, was based on my experience of writing for publications in India, which faced little competition for a reader's attention.

In the big cities in the U.S., up until the early 1990's, there were two or more major newspapers, numerous national and local magazines and several TV channels competing for a reader's attention. In contrast, in major Indian cities, the major English newspaper had a near monopoly of readers.

In Mumbai, for instance, *The Times of India* had a circulation of about 300,000 copies, reaching a small but wealthy audience in the commercial capital of India. On Sundays, some households in Mumbai purchased a second English newspaper, mainly *The Indian Express*, whose circulation was about a third of the *Times*. The TV station and the radio stations in India were then government-run and offered little competition - unless there was a major cricket match.

Most feature stories in *The Times of India* or the Sunday edition of the *Express* were read or at least noticed by English language readers in Mumbai. So the focus for journalists and freelancers was to write about topics that editors liked and not worry much about whether it appealed to readers. The editors of course said that they knew what stories were likely to be popular with their readers.

Print newspaper circulation in India continues to grow, and the business enjoys the best finances in the world, according to the World Association of Newspapers and News Publishers. Print newspapers are still the dominant way to reach consumers in India.

They capture 43% of the revenue spent on advertisements, while television gets about 38%.

Newspaper advertising revenues rose from about $1.2 billion in 2006 to an estimated $3 billion in 2015. Much of the growth is due to Indian language newspapers, which have seen strong growth in circulation. English newspapers have also enjoyed good growth. This is in contrast to the declining revenues and profits of print newspapers in the U.S. and other western countries.

## Caste in America

I did not get good grades and also did not win any awards, even minor ones, at the J School. I also had to take a remedial class on Saturdays for the core Reporting and Writing course, with a few other students. One of my teachers Kathleen Teltsch wrote, "He still needs more confidence," in her assessment of my performance for her UN course.

Only late into the final semester I realized that core courses carried far greater weight in overall academic grades than the minor ones. Until then I assumed all courses carried equal weight, though finding this out earlier would not have mattered, since I did equally poorly in the minor ones.

I rationalized my poor grades and lack of awards by saying I was probably doing OK. Besides writing for *India Abroad*, I had three stories published in U.S. publications, including one about my lost briefcase.

I wrote a story "Indian Immigrants: Keeping Alive the Old Ways in the New Land" for the weekend Long Island section of *The New York Times*. Pranay Gupte, an alumnus of the school, introduced me to the editor of the section, who was one of his former colleagues at the newspaper.

The article, published in 1986 as a full page cover story,

pointed out that the Indians living in Long Island were first generation immigrants. They had moved from Queens, the neighboring New York City borough, upon becoming more affluent, for better schools and housing. Their religious, eating, cultural and social activities continued as if they were living in India, including marrying spouses from their religious, linguistic and caste backgrounds.

As Kamala Narayan, a teacher of Indian classical dance in East Meadow, said, "It's strange. You travel thousands of miles and come here and find the same differences (as in India) between Brahmans and non-Brahmans," Hindus and Muslims, and those from North India and South India. The major exposure to American culture and lifestyle and to other Americans comes when kids start school and their Indian parents meet other parents at school events.

Accompanying the main story was a side-bar on the eight Indian restaurants on Long Island. They included Sitar in Melville started by a husband and wife, both engineers, with the husband a University of Pennsylvania graduate. The editor suggested I write about the restaurants, and I assumed he liked Indian food. He may have wanted to attract the restaurants as advertisers.

While Indian professionals have done well in the U.S., it is unclear if the second generation will be equally successful. Many Indian parents, especially those from the upper castes, do not ask their children to do physical labor even at home, viewing it as low caste work to be done by servants.

Many Indian kids grow up in the U.S. with no experience of working at McDonald's and other similar entry level jobs. Such work is the source of valuable experience and early training for several successful American executives and high achievers.

Perhaps a lack of exposure to minimum wage physical jobs

may not matter much since professional jobs increasingly require advanced intellectual and technical skills, which Indian parents emphasize. But the children of Indian professionals face a major obstacle in getting access to acquiring such skills via top colleges.

The number of Asian students admitted to Ivy League and other top colleges has stayed the same for the past twenty years, despite the rapid rise in the Asian population in the U.S. This fact is often lost in the debate over Tiger parenting by Asians.

"Consider that Asians make up anywhere from 40 to 70 percent of the student population at top public high schools like Stuyvesant and Bronx Science in New York City, Lowell in San Francisco and Thomas Jefferson in Alexandria, Va., where admissions are largely based on exams and grades," wrote Carolyn Chen, director of the Asian American Studies Program at Northwestern University, in an article in *The New York Times* in December 2012 titled "Asians: Too Smart For Their Own Good?"

Yet, as Chen points out, Asian-Americans are only "12 to 18 percent of the student body at Ivy League schools."

If this condition is to be remedied, Indians and other Asian-Americans need to become major donors, join and influence college administrative boards and become vocal lobbyists to get rid of the unofficial quotas at the Ivy League colleges.

## Shaking Hands with Paul McCartney

I assumed I might not be in New York for long and so indulged in a variety of the city's cultural offerings: films, including classics shown at Film Forum, museums, with the Metropolitan continuing to be the favorite, Rudolf Nureyev's "Swan Lake" with the Paris Opera Ballet performed at the Metropolitan Opera House, the New York Philharmonic orchestra led by the Indian conductor Zubin Mehta and several concerts: by Paul McCartney, Pink Floyd, The

Pretenders and others.

A Bruce Springsteen concert was the best, both for his intense performance for three hours and a good view of the stage from an 18th row seat. I got an extra ticket at face value minutes before the concert started. The worst I attended was by the Grateful Dead since it was mostly a long guitar solo followed by a long drum solo. Evidently it was enjoyed by the Deadheads who viewed the series of seven concerts as one continuous musical experience.

The Madison Square Garden venue was thick with smoke, mostly marijuana. Equally bad was a concert by Bob Dylan both for the smoke and since he sings his songs differently than he does on his records. But the air in the Garden for a Neil Diamond concert was smoke-free, and the crowd was mostly women dressed as if out for a formal evening.

I ignored the attitude of many New Yorkers who insist you must leave celebrities alone. I shook hands with Robin Williams, after a Broadway play starring Robert De Niro, not knowing who he was and because classmate Tobie Stanger said I should. I asked Dustin Hoffman, while getting his autograph, what he does when he is not making films. He said he is busy with his kids. I told him and the others that the autographs were for my cousin in Mumbai.

I saw Ringo Starr on Park Avenue and asked him for an autograph. He said OK but I did not have a pen or paper. He joked, asking why then was I seeking an autograph, but waited while I got paper and pen from a doorman nearby.

On a sunny fall afternoon, I saw Paul McCartney about to enter the Bergdorf Goodman store on Fifth Avenue. I went up and told him, "Paul I want to thank you. I enjoyed listening to the Beatles growing up in Mumbai and now my kids listen to your songs." He declined to sign an autograph but shook my hand.

Jim Reisler, a J school classmate, invited me to my first baseball game on opening day in 1986 at Yankee Stadium. He grew up in Pittsburg when the Steelers won the Super Bowl and the

Pirates won the World Series.

I also went with Jim to a minor league baseball game in Reading, Pennsylvania. There I got my first taste of the middle class lifestyle that American politicians claim to be fighting to preserve - families driving up in big cars, easy parking, most fans wearing team T shirts and baseball caps, eating hot dogs and drinking supersize cups of beer and cola while cheering their team.

I saw my only ice hockey game when Jim's dad took us to see the Penguins play, when I visited Jim in Pittsburgh. I realized that goaltenders play a far more important role in ice hockey than they do in field hockey. It was also as difficult to follow the puck as it is to see the ball during a live game in a big field.

### A House Guest for Three Weeks

After graduating from Columbia, I spent three weeks in San Gabriel near Pasadena, California, at the home of classmate Annette Kondo. Annette drove me to the tourist attractions in and around Los Angeles. A special treat was eating Chinese food at places with menus only in Mandarin, with her friends from Hong Kong and Taiwan.

Such long stays with family and friends are common in India, or was common when I lived there. But I realize it may be rare in America. I was reminded of the generosity of the Kondo family when Charles De Souza, visiting from Mumbai, stayed with us in Scarsdale, New York for about three months in 2000.

A neighbor asked why Charles was living with us for so many weeks, implying perhaps that we rented him a room in our house. When I replied he was a close friend, the neighbor asked, "How can you have a friend staying with you for so long?"

From Los Angeles I took a bus along the scenic coastal road

Highway 1 to San Francisco. I stayed with Tom Valtin, a classmate who left the journalism school midway to pursue a career in music.

We paid $5, including tips, for our breakfast of spicy omelets and sausages, with Colombian coffee, at a small restaurant serving Hispanic laborers in the Mission District. Today, the area is booming with offices of technology and social media companies and luxury apartments. It would cost more than $5 to get one cup of good coffee.

When I left India, I had no idea of what I was going to do after finishing from Columbia. While at the journalism school, I applied for several jobs at U.S. publications to get a year's on the job training and also try to pay off my student loans.

I had three interviews and no job offers. One interview was for the post of an editorial writer for *The Waterbury Republican* in Connecticut. Any chance of getting the job was gone after I typed Mrs. instead of Mr. in my thank you note to the editor.

Matt Cain, a classmate, recommended me for a reporter's job at *Electronic News*. The weekly covered the booming computer and information technology business. It was owned by Fairchild Publications, which published several other very profitable trade publications like *Women's Wear Daily* and *Supermarket News*.

The editor said he could not hire me since I did not have a green card or work visa. I got the same answer after meeting with the editor of *Bond Buyer,* following an introduction from Michelle Murphy, another classmate from the journalism school.

I cut my two-page resume into one page since Matt said nobody reads the second page. He also told me that *Forbes* was looking to hire reporters. I read a few issues of the magazine for the first time and wrote and met Jean Briggs, senior editor and the head of reporters. She said there were no current openings.

I tried to get a job at the UN since the pay, health care plans and retirement benefits were very good compared to what even top business executives earned in India. I was told by UN employees that I had no chance since the job quota for Indian men was more than full, though the existence of such national job quotas was not officially acknowledged.

## Chapter 2

## ELEVEN YEARS OF SCHOOL FOR $120

My first teacher was Mom, who ran a kindergarten (KG) class in a room of our row house in Kalina, Mumbai. She was known as Winnie teacher, since her name is Winnie. The class of 20 three- and four-year- olds was filled months in advance; and there was a wait list, reflecting the rising demand for English language education in India.

### Jack and Jill Went up the Hill

The class ran from 9 a.m. to 12 noon, Monday through Saturday, from June to April. Mom taught by what she considered the Montessori system. Each morning, while a few kids cried on being separated from their mothers and grandmothers, Mom would start the class by singing and acting out nursery rhymes. The first and most popular rhyme was:

"Jack and Jill went up the hill
To fetch a pail of water,
Jack fell down
And broke his crown
And Jill came tumbling after."

Other nursery rhymes included "Baa Baa Black Sheep," "Pat A Cake," "Little Miss Muffett," and "Hey Diddle Diddle," inherited from the days of British rule in India. The content of most of these rhymes will be considered politically incorrect these days.

After the nursery rhymes, mom led a reciting of alphabets: A is for apple, B is for bird and so on. Some of the words, including in the nursery rhymes like "whey" and "fiddle," were objects only seen as images in books, not being used or seen in India.

The class was the first exposure to English for many of the kids, who were from families which spoke Gujarati, Hindi or Marathi. Perhaps the English words and images of unseen objects helped a few kids expand their imagination.

Around 10.30 a.m., there was a break for tiffin, snacks the kids brought from home. They reflected the regional backgrounds with South Indians eating idlis and vadas and Gujaratis having chewda, a spicy mix of roasted rice, raisins and nuts.

After tiffin, Mom taught the kids to write on a slate with a stick of chalk. The slate was a thin flat mined stone, with wooden strips covering the edges and a handle made of wire. It was assumed that kids are right-handed, and so many left-handed kids learned to write using their right hand. They started with the easier capital letters for alphabets.

As the year progressed, the kids were taught to recite numbers, starting with 1 to 10. They were then taught to write numbers and simple words such as cat and hat. A few progressed to simple addition and subtraction and writing longer words.

Until this day I don't know what is the Montessori system and if Mom followed it. By age four I knew my alphabets, could write small words and recite numbers. I was a teacher's aide, serving water during tiffin breaks and helping kids with their work.

From 2:00 p.m. to 5:00 p.m., Mom tutored six to eight elementary and middle school students. She ran the KG class and tutored in part to supplement Dad's income. She also had several interests, like learning to knit woolen sweaters using patterns and instructions from *Woman & Home*, a British magazine.

### Dad's Real Estate Strategy

When my parents moved to Kalina in the early 1950's, it was a remote suburb of Mumbai. Dad worked for Air India, India's international airlines. It was owned by the Tata Group and later taken over by the government. The Mumbai airport terminal and the hangars for repairing and housing planes, for Air India and the domestic carrier Indian Airlines, were based around Kalina.

Kalina was a wooded area with jackals, foxes and wolves. Relatives and friends would often recount the story of how Dad killed a porcupine with his lathi, a solid wooden pole he kept behind the front door.

One evening, when I was about four years old, I was sucking my left thumb and seated on Dad's feet while he read the *Times of India*. A snake slithered by inches from me, having come through the door on our left that opened on to the back yard. I quietly pointed it out to Dad.

He got up, picked his pole and hit the snake in the middle of its back and then killed it with a hit to its head. Dad explained that he learnt the technique while growing up in Kerala, a Southern Indian state with cobras, vipers and kraits: you first paralyze the snake by breaking its back and then kill it. If you first aim for the head and miss, then the snake can bite you.

I used the technique a few years later to kill a green vine snake. The thin snake, with a diamond shaped head and mildly venomous, had slid down from a tree near where I was sitting and eating raw tamarind.

Many of dad's colleagues rented apartments from Air India, which built a housing complex of several modern buildings with three floors, gardens and a soccer field in Kalina. These colleagues had to move out when they retired from Air India in the 1980s. Some of them had bought apartments in Kalina, paying over a hundred times what it cost in the 1950s. The children of other colleagues had to find jobs in Air India, so the family could continue to live in the company apartments.

Our house, at the corner of a four-unit row house with a sloping roof, had a yard on three sides and faced a garden. It was in a housing complex of 192 homes called Sundar Nagar, or Beautiful Town, built in the early 1950s by the Maharashtra state government for middle income households, what the British call public sector middle class. The monthly rent was about Rs. 60, or $10, and the ownership was transferred to the tenants in the 1970s.

Dad and Joseph, my younger brother, planted rose, jasmine and sunflower bushes in the front yard. I planted vegetable seeds in May, before the start of the monsoon rains. By August we had beans, pumpkins, green chili peppers and tomatoes.

In the back there was a large guava tree and a Curry Leaf tree, whose leaves were sold to a vegetable vendor. Dad planted four mango trees along the outer edges of the side yard. We got to enjoy different types of mangos, though one summer a local gang of youths stole most of the fruit.

Real estate prices have boomed in Mumbai, more so than in most major Indian cities. There is limited supply in Mumbai, in addition to demand from a growing population, rising incomes and impact of inflation. The city is an island with the main part being 26 square miles and the suburban area another 143 square miles, while the population is over 20 million.

The offices of Microsoft, Rolls Royce engines and other major cvompanies are located in Kalina, which is three miles from the Bandra Kurla complex, the new commercial center of Mumbai.

Neighbors who held onto the row houses in Sundar Nagar have seen values rise over 20,000 fold. The single floor units have been converted into multi-floor homes, some with multiple apartments and multi-car garages, selling for $400 per square foot.

### Gaining a Year in School

I was admitted to the first grade at St. Mary's High School in Kalina, a day school for boys and girls. I knew my alphabets and numbers, and my February birthday met the cut-off date. Most students, including my two brothers and sister who were born later in the year, had to spend a year in Kindergarten.

I was proud to be the second youngest student in my grade. I should have been humble. Later I lost two years in college when I switched from chemistry to philosophy and another year when I did not get my M.Phil. admission letter.

I did not cry on my first day of school, after my older brother George left me in my classroom. He was in third grade. (He passed away some years ago.)

My first grade teacher's nickname was "buddi" (old) teacher. Senior students competed to come up with popular nicknames for new teachers.

She was the oldest teacher at the school, with a bent back, gray unruly hair, a few wisps of gray beard on her chin, a loud raspy voice and dressed in long skirts. She enforced discipline by caning students with a wooden measuring ruler.

# ELEVEN YEARS OF SCHOOL FOR $120

St. Mary's is a private-public hybrid, like many schools in India. It is run by the Catholic church, which also owns the building. The government sets the fees, pays the wages of the teachers and staff, sets the curriculum and selects the textbooks.

My school fees were five Rupees a month for the first grade. It rose to Rs.11 per month in my eleventh grade. The total cost of my eleven years of schooling was about nine hundred Rupees or $120. Education in India is heavily subsidized by the government.

St. Mary's, founded in 1876, was housed in a long school building, with three floors. The class rooms were used in two shifts, with middle and high school classes in the morning and elementary school classes in the afternoon.

The building is attached to the Church of Our Lady of Egypt, which was founded in 1606. There was a large yard in front of the school and another behind the church, covered with headstones of burial plots.

My first grade classroom overlooked an athletic and soccer field. It was fenced in by high brick walls, topped with barbed wire. The church owned a larger field where the school's annual sports meet was held during my first grade.

One night several huts were built on the field by a group led by a local mafia don who must have bribed politicians, the police and bureaucrats. The church effectively lost the land since court judgements in such civil cases take several decades and are difficult to implement due to opposition from politicians.

Students and parents wondered why the church officials failed to put up a fence and protect ownership of the field.

## Troubles with Water Lilies

The front yard of St. Mary's school faced a rectangular pond of about twenty acres, with white and pink water lilies, which we ignorantly but proudly called lotus. Residents in the huts nearby bathed and washed their clothes in the pond.

During a recess in the second grade, I climbed down to the edge of the pond, through an opening in the barbed-wire fence, to pluck a white lily.

I got the lily, but my trousers got wet. I was hoping it would dry before I got home. But Dennis, a classmate who encouraged me to get the lily, told our teacher. She sent me home.

Dad was angry since I risked physical harm. He did not let me play cricket for a week.

At school there were tests every six weeks, a mid-year exam in October and a final exam in April. The tests and the midyear exam counted for 20%, and the final exam for 80% of the grade in each course.

The time allotted to the final exams rose from an hour in elementary school to three hours in the 11th grade. We had to memorize much of the texts for the courses to be able to answer the exam questions.

I passed the major courses and was ranked 14 out of 56 students in my second grade division. When Dad asked why I had not gotten a higher rank, I said it was better than most of my classmates. He got angry and said I should aim to do better, not compare myself with those who have done worse.

That summer, during the monsoon season, I fell into a stream on the far side of the garden, across from our house. I was trying to jump over the stream, being chased by a farmer for picking lettuce from his field.

I had read that rabbits like lettuce and wanted to get fresh ones for my rabbit. I washed the mud off my hands and feet, in the backyard of a school nearby. Suresh, a kid living near us, asked what I was doing. I told him what happened, and he went and told Dad and some other kids.

Besides rabbits, I kept fishes, parrots, lovebirds, mynah and squirrels. We also had ducks and chickens. I would not eat the meat of the ducks and chickens I fed, when they were cooked, and my parents respected my decision.

I wanted more pets and so spent hours making cages with wood slats and wire meshing, during the summer school break.

In third grade I saw some rare pink lilies in the middle of the small row boat used by school and church employees. The boat was tied to a landing at the edge of the pond. I climbed into the boat to get a pink lily. A student, whose identity I never found out, pushed the boat into the water.

I was in the boat, about 15 feet from the landing. I did not know how to swim. Hundreds of students stopped their games and chatting to watch me upon hearing shouts from the landing.

Andrew, a 10th grade student, top athlete and an easy going friendly person, waded thigh deep into the water. I caught the pole he held out, and he pulled the boat back to the landing.

I told my brother George he could have any of my books and games if he did not tell our parents about my adventure. But Bruno, a student my Mom tutored, told her. I lost more cricket playing time, among other punishments from Dad.

I also had troubles with bicycles. In first grade, Dad would often give me a ride home on the back seat of his Raleigh ladies bicycle. One evening, I cried out loudly, just after we left the school gates. I had put my left heel into the spokes of the bicycle wheel. A square inch scar reminds me of the accident to this day.

During third grade, I was playing on the street in front of my house when a high school bully lost control of his speeding bicycle and ran over my right foot.

A few years later, after learning to ride, my bicycle hit an old lady crossing the street, in front of the police booth at the Kalina bazaar.

### Imagining the Taste of Buttered Scones

The school year was long, from June to April. The homeroom teacher taught all the courses during my first four grades. I had OK teachers, with little interest in students, except for my third grade teacher who was gentle and encouraging.

I liked reading and spent hours each day going through newspapers, books and magazines, including *TIME*, *LIFE* and *Readers' Digest*, which we borrowed from a neighbor.

I had no interest when Dad read aloud Arthur Conan Doyle's Sherlock Holmes stories. I also did not like murder mysteries, horror stories, science fiction, gear head magazines like *Popular Mechanics* as well as Superman, Batman and other super character comics.

My favorite character was William, the freckled, red-haired 11-year-old in Richmal Crompton's books. He got into trouble as he and his friends tried to help others, including trying to find a husband for his older sister.

I read most of the storybooks by Crompton and Enid

Blyton, both British authors, which were in the school library. I wondered what buttered scones tasted like, which were enjoyed by the kids in Enid Blyton's books.

The school library had only children's fiction books. There were no public libraries in Kalina and only a handful in Mumbai. There were three for-profit local libraries. They charged a monthly membership fee and a fee per book or magazine borrowed. The best one was run by an English woman, married to an Indian, who ran the business from her apartment.

Mom borrowed books and comics from her and also bought illustrated books like *Knowledge*, which covered science, history and geography. I also liked reading *Sad Sack, Mickey Mouse, Uncle Scrooge* and *Archie* comics and the Phantom stories, about a masked man helping the pygmies in Africa.

The Phantom comic books, published by *The Times of India*, had a cartoon strip on the last page. One cartoon showed a big, muscular man lifting increasingly heavier weights, one by one. He proudly bows to the audience, with a thin small man next to him, in the second to last frame. In the final frame, the muscle man walks away waving, followed by the small man carrying all the weights under his thin arms.

## Chapter 3

# LOSING SANTA CLAUS IN MUMBAI

I was close to my maternal grandparents and my Mom's two sisters. They too lived in Kalina, on the edge of a military camp, set on a hill by the British, with rest houses, training and medical facilities. The camp, of several hundred acres, was wooded with lots of Banyan, tamarind and mango trees.

I spent several hot, sweaty summer days in the shade of the Banyan and tamarind trees. I swung from the hanging roots of the Banyan trees. I would throw stones to knock down tamarind and mangoes. I vainly waited for parrots, mynahs and squirrels to be caught by my traps, which were traps meant for catching rats that I had slightly modified.

### My Favorite Beatle: George Harrison

Dada, as we called our maternal grandfather, was nearly blind due to cataract problems. Yet he walked on his own to church every morning. A thin, erect and bald man, who enjoyed walking, he spoke very little. He was cheated out of his ancestral lands, but he never complained or pined for what might have been. He sat in an easy chair under the shade of a tamarind tree, smoking a locally made cigar.

Once or twice a year he would disappear for weeks saying he was setting up business deals. Nothing resulted from these trips, at least financially, though he brought sweets and fruits. Our aunts would tell stories about Dada's meetings with famous people during his trips.

Aunt Suzy helped organize meetings and charity drives for the local chapter of the Young Women's Christian Association. Aunt Philo was a good student and athlete and played the violin. Both of them took my siblings and me to attend cultural and athletic events and their company picnics, which opened up a wider world.

I listened to English pop music at their home through radio broadcasts and vinyl records played on a HMV gramophone, a large box with a speaker and a hand cranked turntable.

I would tune in to Radio Ceylon most evenings, on an old, shortwave Murphy radio, to listen to an hour-long broadcast of pop songs. I also listened to the weekly BBC program "Top of the Pops," and I wrote and got a program button.

The Beatles were my favorite band and George Harrison my favorite Beatle. I looked forward to new songs from the Beatles. So, when the band split, I was hoping they would get back together. To this day, I start work every morning by listening to Harrison singing "Here Comes the Sun".

**Finding Bargains in a Mumbai Bazaar**

My siblings and I walked to school, sometimes with classmates and friends. Grandma and Mom reminded us to avoid talking to strangers and told us stories of kids being kidnapped.

I would run when I saw the Hijras. A group of them, in brightly colored saris and heavy makeup, show up and dance to loud singing and clapping, outside a home where a child is born or there is a wedding. They go away only if they are satisfied with the "baksheesh" or gift of money.

The Hijras get the information on births and weddings from the local municipal offices. In 2014, the Indian Supreme Court granted third gender status to the Hijras, eunuchs, intersex or transgendered people. This enables them to be admitted to medical and other professional colleges and get government and semi-government jobs through reserved quotas.

Grandma and my aunts would poke fun of my fear of the "Googo Bayl," a bull covered with bright colored sheets and with bells in its horns. The rural soothsayer who walked alongside the bull, dressed in a dhoti, kurta and a white turban, would rub a stick on his dholak, or Indian drum, proclaiming in Hindi "children will pass their exams" and "family will be healthy." He would go away only after he got a payment. I hid under the bed and emerged only after I no longer heard the sound of the drum.

My Grandma did our shopping since Mom was busy teaching. She would often take me along to the Kalina bazaar, an open air market run by the city government. At one end were the male Muslim vendors of beef and lamb, with flanks of meat hanging from hooks. In the middle were vendors of fresh and dried fish, women who were East Indians or Kolis, and also vendors of vegetables, fruits and flowers, Hindu Maharashtrian women from the Mali or gardener caste. At the other end of the bazaar were the Muslim vendors of chickens and eggs.

At the back of the bazaar were the restrooms. Standing or seated nearby were those who cleaned the bazaar, mostly women from the scheduled castes. They smoked bidis, crude cigarettes of tobacco wrapped in a tobacco leaf - the only women I saw smoking in public in India till I went to college.

The prices of beef and lamb were fixed because the vendors

enjoyed a monopoly, though there was some bargaining for better cuts based on quantity purchased and frequency of purchases. There was lots of bargaining for fish, vegetables and flowers since there were several vendors and the items were perishable. The fish were kept cold in baskets of ice chips and had to be sold by the end of the day.

Grandma shopped at only a few of the vendors whom she knew had quality products at good prices, based on her history of previous purchases.

She would ask a vendor for the price of a pomfret fish after checking the weight and the gills for freshness. If the vendor said six rupees, Grandma would say she bought one last week for four rupees. The vendor would reply that there was a small catch of the fish last night.

Grandma would give five rupees to the vendor if she thought the fish was a good deal. Most of the time the vendor would take the money and put the fish in her shopping bag. At times Grandma would walk away, and the vendor would call her back saying, "OK I will take four rupees."

Decades later in New York, I realized that I got my early lessons on value investing in stocks from watching Grandma find good bargains.

### Muslim and Jewish Friends

As I walked to St. Mary's school, in my ironed gray shorts and white shirt, red tie with a blue badge and polished black Bata leather shoes, I would pass kids in crumpled khaki shorts and white shirts and cheap sandals on their way to the municipal school. It was run by the Mumbai City administration, admitted all applicants, was free and the education was in Marathi, the language of the state of Maharashtra of which Mumbai is the capital.

The municipal students were from families who lived in well-built huts in and around Kalina. Their mothers cooked, cleaned and hand washed clothes in nearby middle class homes. They were called servants by their employers and were from the scheduled, or lower, castes. Some of the parents, mostly men, worked as peons serving tea, moving paper files and ushering in visitors in government and private offices.

Parents of most municipal school students could afford the small fees at St. Mary's, but getting admitted into such English language schools was very difficult. The demand was so high that three new English high schools were set up in Kalina during the 1960s, including one for girls by the Catholic Church.

Further along on my walk to the school, near the Kalina bazaar, I would pass Muslim kids dressed in kurta and pajamas, with older girls covering their head with cheap green or blue nylon scarves. They were on their way to the Madrasa, or religious school, at the Mosque near the bazaar. The Muslims, seeking to protect themselves during the regular Hindu-Muslim clashes, live in concentrated pockets in Mumbai and elsewhere in India.

Kalina had a large Muslim population, most of them poor. Only a few Muslims studied at St. Mary's school, mostly from professional or small business families like my mother's friends Munira and Farida and their brothers. They offered almonds and cashews, as my siblings and I sat on a large swing which hung in their living room, while visiting them.

While some Muslims are hired by a few private companies, notably those run by the Parsis, very few get government jobs. Some government departments, under Prime Minister Narendra Modi, explicitly state they will not recruit Muslims.

In 2015, for instance, no Muslims were hired as Yoga teachers by a government agency from among 3,800 Muslims who applied. Agency officials said that because of a government policy: "no Muslim candidate was invited."

Most Muslim men work as bakers, butchers, laborers and in small stores repairing umbrellas and stoves and other gadgets. Some Muslim women work as cooks, baby sitters and cleaners.

On Sunday mornings, while I was on my way to church, I would come across members of the Rashtriya Swayamsevak Sangh (RSS). They wore khaki shorts, white shirts and black caps and carried a wooden pole, on their way to physical drills at the field next to the municipal school.

They RSS members included several neighbors who were Maharashtrian Brahmans, working for Air India and Indian Airlines. These Hindus refused to let Muslims buy homes in the housing complex where I grew up.

The RSS is a secretive Hindu organization whose member Nathuram Godse shot and killed Mahatma Gandhi in 1948 for making too many concessions to Muslims in post Independent India. The Indian Prime Minister Narendra Modi started his political career as a member of the RSS.

There were also some Jewish families in Kalina, including Speechley, a colleague and friend of Dad at Air India. His wife worked as an administrator at a multi-national corporation.

They invited us to Passover meals at his parents' apartment in Byculla, which then had a big Jewish population. I ate my first large naan breads at these meals, fresh from Muslim-run bakeries.

The Speechley's older daughter wore stylish dresses and shoes. She was three years older than me and the only one I knew in Kalina studying at a private residential school.

Few parents in Kalina could afford to send their children to private schools. Some were interested but did not know how to get admission and scholarships.

Most successful Indian professionals do not share with other parents how they got their children admitted to good private high schools in India as well as into good American and British universities. This is likely because they do not want their children to face more competition for such admissions.

### A Catholic Outsider in a Catholic School

Christians were in a minority at St. Mary's School. For instance, only eleven of the 48 students in my tenth grade class were Christians, while two were Muslims and the rest Hindus.

The Christians in Kalina were mostly Catholics. The majority of Catholics were East Indians, natives of Maharashtra converted by the Portuguese, who first landed in Mumbai in the Sixteenth century.

The East Indians owned land and houses, having been farmers for generations, and many lived on rental income. Several good athletes at my school were East Indians, including two classmates and friends Procter and Conrad.

The other Catholics were from Goa, Mangalore and Kerala, regions south of Mumbai on the Arabian Sea coast. Some Goans were fairer in skin color and claimed to be of Portuguese ancestry. The Goans saw themselves as being at the top of the Catholic social hierarchy in the city.

The Catholics and other Christians from Kerala use an ancestral family name as their last name. But Dad and his two brothers were upset with some family members over a land dispute involving their grandfather.

They decided to use Chithelen as the family name, derived from the Malayalam nickname given to their grandfather for his pursuit of those he felt had cheated or harmed him. Malayalam is the language of Kerala state.

My baptism certificate lists Dad's family name as Maliakal. It also states that I was the thirteenth child to be baptized at the church in the year of my birth.

This may be why I try to benefit from popular fears of the number 13, especially Friday the 13$^{th}$. I submitted forms for my driver's license, U.S. green card and citizenship applications on the 13th day of a month, since there are few people waiting in line.

The head and key staff of St. Mary's school were priests from Our Lady of Egypt church. There was a daily religion class for Catholic students and a course on moral science, or ethics, for the non-Catholics. The religion class was taught by priests and consisted of prayers and lectures based on readings from the Bible and the scriptures.

The vicar, or head priest of the parish, was a short, bald and stern man, in his 70s. He walked with the help of a cane and smoked cigars. He taught the religion class in my high school years.

He shouted at students who talked during his class, which was held in the church. He told a story of how lightning struck and killed an unmarried couple who were committing mortal sin. I failed the religion class in both middle and high school.

There were Catechism classes at the church on Sunday afternoon. Attendance was required for those wanting to receive Holy Communion, usually at age 7, and Confirmation around age 12. The teachers were priests, Catholic teachers and parents.

## A Teacher Sweats as Santa Claus

Each year the church held a Christmas party for the Catholic students. There were snacks - samosas and batata vadas - balloons, an artificial Christmas tree decorated with colored lights, and a Santa Claus.

During the Christmas party in second grade, I heard my brother George and his friends discuss that the Santa Claus was Mr. Paul. I went and peered up close at Santa Claus but did not recognize Mr.Paul, a physical education teacher.

When I said this to George, he took me to the teacher's common room and asked me to peek in. I saw Mr. Paul, who had taken off the white beard and red hat, seated in the red Santa robe and chatting with the other teachers.

He fit the image of a Santa Claus, a jovial man with a big paunch, though the Santa suit, hat and beard made him sweat a lot in the heat and humidity of Mumbai.

Mr. Paul was one of the few teachers who was so well liked that he was not given a nickname by the students. He was friendly and easy going. When we made an error, he smiled and asked us to repeat an exercise. He did not cane us or ask us to do push-ups, like the other physical education teachers who were former army soldiers. He was also lenient about the physical exercises, letting us play soccer or other games for over half the allotted time.

During the week before Christmas, my siblings and I would help Mom and Grandma make special snacks, mostly fried and sugar-coated white flour of different shapes. My favorite sweet was a pound cake with raisins and dried fruit bought from a bakery. I did not care for the pork, potato and other specialties at Christmas meals. My favorite dish continues to be eggs sunny side up.

On Christmas Day, Mom would fill up a plate with snacks and my siblings and I would give them to neighbors and friends, Hindus, Muslims and Jews. The content showed the degree of friendship, with close family friends getting a bigger plate with the best sweets. Hindu neighbors and friends would bring us a plate of sweets and snacks, during Diwali, the festival of lights.

Dad was an atheist who rarely went to church. He admired the sparse life and missionary work among the poor of the Franciscan and Capuchin monks. I grew up as an outsider, a Keralite minority among the Catholics, with an atheist dad, and a Catholic minority among Hindus.

Christians, though only 2% of the population, play an important role in India. Julio Ribeiro, a former police chief of Mumbai wrote in *The Indian Express* in 2015, following attacks on Christian churches by Hindu fundamentalists in Delhi, "Christians have consistently punched above their weight – not as much as the tiny Parsi community in India, but just as noticeably...Many schools, colleges and establishments teach that teach skills for jobs have been set up and run by Christians. They are much in demand. Even diehard Hindus have sought admission in such centers of learning and benefited from the commitment and sincerity of Christian teachers...Hospitals, nursing homes, hospices for dying cancer patients needing palliative care – many of these are run by Christian religious orders or Christian laymen devoted to the service of humanity."

# Chapter 4

# REACH FOR THE SKY

My school hours were from 7:30 a.m. to 1:00 p.m. from fifth grade onwards. Upon returning home from school, I ate lunch and climbed the guava tree in the back yard. I sat on a sturdy branch in the shade, ate guavas, read books and comics and day dreamed.

I went back into the house, after about half an hour, and did my homework. From 5:00 p.m. till about 6:30 p.m., I played cricket with a group of boys living nearby. We played soccer, during the monsoon season from June to August, getting wet and covered in dirt and suffering injuries.

I was the captain of our cricket and soccer teams since the bat, wickets and balls were bought by Dad. We played matches against other teams but lost most of them. During breaks, the Brahman boys held a stainless steel glass about three inches above their mouths and then poured the water to quench their thirst. They did not want their lips to touch the glasses used by boys from the other castes.

### My Favorite School Teacher

I looked forward to going to school in the fifth grade. My teacher was Ms. Annie, who brought up current events related to the history, geography and civics topics she was teaching. She encouraged questions and discussions, and I was eager to answer her questions. She often said, "If you reach for the sky, you will at least touch the tree-tops."

She wore skirts and blouses and dresses with floral prints, unlike most other women teachers who wore saris. Her thick curly black hair, cut in a neat bob, framed her high cheek bones, and her dark eyes sparkled with enthusiasm.

I was proud when Ms. Annie appointed me head of the Blue House. All students were assigned to Blue, Brown, Green and Red houses in the first grade. The houses competed in athletics and elocution contests.

Each house had an annual party, with plays, musical performances, bingo and samosas. Joseph, a classmate and son of the biggest real estate developer in Kalina, said he was going to sing at the Blue House party. I said I would join him even though I had a bad voice and never played a guitar.

We got on stage and sang "Woolly Bully," by Sam the Sham and the Pharaohs, with me using one of Joseph's guitars. A string on my guitar broke midway through the song. Joseph was upset but did not ask me to pay for a new set of strings, which I assumed would be expensive.

A student, whom Mom tutored, told her that I broke Joseph's guitar. She was very angry and shouted, "We ants don't beg, borrow or steal." I was so shaken by the incident and Mom's reaction that I was afraid to go back onto a public stage until I got to college.

On the last day of school, Ms. Annie said the student who ranked third in the division is a surprise. He is quiet in class and has shown good improvement. I wondered who was the student. She announced my name, and I was happy but surprised - since I had ranked 18 out of 62 students in the mid-year exam.

I got over 60% in geography, English, science and history. I just managed to pass in fine arts, crafts and physical education, which were not included for the ranking. My report stated that I was 4 feet 3 inches tall and weighed 46 pounds.

That day in April 1965 was also a sad one because it was Ms. Annie's last day at the school. She married an army officer and moved to Pune. She was my favorite teacher in school.

### Falling Into a Barrel of Hooch

**M**y fifth grade report card noted that I missed eight of 235 school days that year. This was because Dad had been in the hospital for two weeks due to a heart problem.

Each day he smoked over fifty strong, unfiltered Charminar cigarettes and also chewed a dozen paans, which had tobacco, areca nuts and chunam mixed in a betel leaf.

I did not fully grasp the gravity of his condition and continued with my cricket games. One day, in his room at the Bombay Hospital, he asked why I had not visited him earlier and if I did not care what happened. It was the only time he showed such emotions. Like other Indian Dads, and perhaps most men, he tried to shield his children from his problems.

Dad stopped chewing paan and switched to smoking filtered Wills cigarettes when he got out of the hospital. Some months later he stopped smoking, but it would be too late.

That summer I slipped and fell into a hole in the ground filled with dirty, stinking water. I was playing a cop chasing robbers. Barrels of bewda, or illicitly made alcohol, were stored in the hole for fermenting.

I took a long shower and soaped myself several times in the nearby yard of a friend. He was the only other Ignatius who I knew in Mumbai. Yet, when I got home, Mom asked why I smelled.

Kalina was known in Mumbai for its high quality illegal liquor. Every few months the police raided the illegal dens, took away the barrels and arrested the operators. They would be back in business, with a new set of barrels, a few days later.

The riskiest of my water adventures was on a pond formed by the accumulation of rainwater. Water hyacinths covered much of the pond in August, near the end of the monsoon.

I would join several kids piling up the hyacinths to make floating rafts. We climbed on the rafts and floated in the pond. The rafts would disintegrate, due to the weight of the kids, and we fell into the water. Luckily the rafts did not travel far and, not knowing how to swim, we walked back to the edge of the pond. But my troubles with water continued into adult life.

### Interest in a Merchant Navy Career

The sixth grade teacher was tall, slender, good looking and wore colored chiffon saris. But she was angry and had a cynical laugh. She taught for only a few minutes and then chatted with teachers and priests. She was only nice to students whose parents had money and influence in the school and church.

She asked me to stand outside the classroom on several occasions and asked a parent to meet her to discuss my bad behavior. This was the only time my Dad, or Mom, visited the school to meet with a teacher. Each day I went to school fearing what the teacher would do next.

My seventh grade teacher was Mr. Rodriguez. He was nicknamed "Matkya", or pot, because he had a pot shaped belly, covered by his untucked bright checked shirts. He was bald, in his fifties, with a few clumps of unruly gray hair and the middle finger of his left hand was twisted sideways.

Mr. Rodriguez was a history teacher. To this day I recall his discussion of Muhammad ibn Tughluq, a fourteenth century king. He tried to shift the capital of his empire from Delhi to a new city in Southern India, which was more centrally located. The residents of Delhi refused his orders to move.

Tughluq got his treasury to mint copper coins, which were exchangeable for existing silver ones. Soon the treasury's silver coins were gone, replaced with a large pile of copper coins, bankrupting his kingdom.

Matkya got angry when he was disturbed while teaching. He used the wooden handle of a duster to rap the knuckles of the offending male students. I did not mind such punishment because Matkya treated all students equally.

He was also generous, buying samosas for the students once a month. He did this while supporting a mother on a salary that was less than what a bank clerk made.

Most of my school classmates wanted to get a college degree and work in public sector jobs, like their fathers, at Air India, Indian Airlines, banks, insurance and other government-run companies. A few of the more ambitious ones wanted to become architects, doctors or engineers.

I had no career goal until I got to the seventh grade. Then, during a visit to an Indian Navy ship, I imagined sailors lived an attractive life of fun travel and independence.

I decided to become a merchant navy officer since the wages were better than in the Indian Navy. I planned to take the competitive entrance exam for admission to a four-year program on a training ship anchored in Mumbai harbor after finishing my tenth grade.

I got 80% in arithmetic and was ranked fourth in my division of 44 students in seventh grade. There was a sharp decline in the size of classes, from five divisions, with about 60 students each in the first grade, to two divisions with about 45 students each in the eleventh grade. This was because of the high failure rate.

Students who got less than 35%, in three or more major courses, were failed and had to repeat the school year. A few would repeat, facing taunts from new classmates, and try to pass the exams. But most of the failing students moved to a less rigorous school and some quit school.

### Where There is a Will There is a Way

I joined the Road Safety Patrol (RSP). We wore bright red hats, had whistles and directed pedestrian and vehicle traffic after school ended. The students ignored us and called us Ragda Samosa Patties, after three Indian snacks.

Earlier I had volunteered with Mom when she was a civil defense warden, during the 1965 India Pakistan war. We walked around our housing complex to check there were no lights visible from the outside, on nights when sirens warned of threats from Pakistani aircraft.

The RSP volunteers helped control crowds at major public events. My favorite was the annual fair at Mount Mary's church in Bandra, held in September. I got to hear local rock bands performing in a couple of the tents.

We traveled on buses and trains to RSP events like marching competitions and rallies. On one trip, I squeezed into a crowded train car at Santacruz station and tightly held the pole at the entrance.

The train started and the kids, who were on the platform, shouted that I should get down. I jumped and was lucky to be caught in the air by Anthony, the school's RSP leader and shot put champion. I would have gotten hurt if I had fallen on the platform since the train had picked up speed.

During the five-week summer break between school years, my parents, siblings and I visited Dad's family in Kerala. We mostly stayed at his father's house in Irinjalakuda, a small town in the central part of the state. There was a room at the back of the house, whose floor was covered with rice paddy, where mangoes and jackfruits were stored for ripening.

We also visited Dad's brothers and sisters. One uncle, married to Dad's oldest sister, taught at Maharaja's College in Ernakulam, one of the best in the state. He was a bald, tall and stern man who greeted visitors briefly and then headed back to work in his study.

He tutored Unni, the younger son of Dad's older brother. Unni was tall, light skinned and had no mustache, unlike most Indian men. His dad was a doctor and his mother was the head of athletics at Maharaja's College, perhaps the only woman in such a role in Kerala.

But Unni had no interest in school and got into arguments with teachers and administrators. He was studying to take an entrance exam for admission to an aircraft technicians program. One morning, as he was leaving, Unni got into an argument. The uncle, visibly annoyed, shouted after him, "Where there is a will, there is a way."

I liked Unni, and so did my Dad. One year he took me to a Hindu temple near his home where we fed baby elephants a pudding made of jackfruit pulp. When he moved to England in the 1960s, he mailed Dad *National Geographic* magazines with holes in the pages holding 7 o'clock double-edged razor blades. This was one luxury Dad enjoyed, having gotten used to it while in the U.K.

## Chapter 5

## AN ACCIDENT FINISHING HIGH SCHOOL?

In high school, I figured I had to only get 50% in the 10th grade exams and then join the merchant navy training program. So I had little interest in my studies and neglected the rising workload from the new courses of algebra, geometry, chemistry and physics.

### My Worst Year in School

I was eager to learn to play the guitar. I wanted to socialize with a group of Catholic students, most of whom shunned me. They listened to rock music, chatted about Hollywood movies and read mystery novels by James Hadley Chase. Their goal was to get a college degree and find jobs in Saudi Arabia, Dubai and Bahrain, where the wages were over ten-fold higher and there were no income taxes.

Dad asked me to stay away from the group, saying "an idle mind is a devil's workshop." I ignored him, thinking I was not influenced by the group since I did not smoke and drink alcohol with them.

I got below 50% in the ninth grade, the low point of my school education. I failed in Hindi, Marathi and French, having trouble with languages and the rules of grammar. Only two of these languages, and English, were required for the final high school exam in grade 11. So I did not have to repeat the ninth grade, though I failed three major courses.

I took a tutoring class in Hindi, with 30 other students, to improve my grade. It was taught by Mrs. Rao and the fee was Rs.10, or $1.50, a month.

The Hindi text books had stories and essays and the stories about Birbal were very popular. He was the Hindu chief adviser to the Mughal King Akbar, who ruled much of Northern India from 1556 to his death in 1605.

One story is about King Akbar holding a contest to see if anyone could stand in the lake near the palace during a winter night. A poor farmer managed this feat but was denied the reward of 100 gold coins. The King agreed with an adviser who said the peasant got warmth from the rays of a lamp in the palace.

Birbal did not appear at the King's court for several days, saying he was busy cooking Khichdi, a rice dish. The King visited Birbal and asked if he had gone mad. The pot of rice hung near the ceiling while the fire was on the ground. Birbal respectfully said the rice should cook, just as the light from a lamp kept a peasant warm in freezing water. The King smiled and asked a courier to give the peasant 100 gold coins.

Munshi Premchand wrote *Shatranj Ke Khilari*, the chess players. It is about two nobles in the service of the last Mughal King to rule India. They continue with their chess matches while the British army is preparing to invade the Kingdom.

A film by Satyajit Ray, based on Premchand's story, is a classic of Hindi, non-Bollywood cinema.

In another story, a group of teenage boys place a banana skin on a sidewalk. They distract pedestrians to make them slip on the skin. The pedestrians get up embarrassed and angry and the boys laugh loudly.

Then one man slips and gets up but ignores the boys and continues. The boys are quiet. The moral of the story is that if you accept your accidents and mistakes, others cannot take advantage.

The Hindi stories also had insightful idioms: a monkey will never grasp the subtle taste of ginger, meaning do not waste time trying to explain something important to a person who will never get it. The one who wields the big stick owns the buffalo, meaning the one who has the financial and political power will control the outcome of a conflict.

In tenth grade, I was chosen to be on a team of four students who represented the school at an inter-school general knowledge competition.

Such contests were popular among English language students due to the weekly Bournvita Quiz contest, named after a chocolate-flavored energy drink sold by Cadbury's. The contest was broadcast over the radio; it is now shown on a TV channel.

Our school team won no awards at the contest held at St. Xavier's College. I did not know why iron sinks in water but floats in mercury. I got the answer from Dad after I got home.

I decided I would go to St. Xavier's if I went to college. I was impressed by the students who ran the contest and liked the campus, with its stone buildings and large yards. It was run by Jesuit priests and was one of the best colleges in Mumbai.

### Dad's Heart Attack

On the night of my 15th birthday, in February 1970, I went to a fair at a church nearby. Dad gave me permission to go, at the urging of Mom. He had returned that day, after spending a week in

Kerala, to attend the funeral of his older brother who died of a heart attack.

At the fair, a pop singer Ajit Singh sang his signature song, "Take off your clothes and let me see what you are hiding…" I got home at 10 p.m., the first time Dad allowed me to stay out so late.

The next morning, around 5.30 am, Dad woke up saying he had a pain in his chest. He lay down and died of a heart attack.

There was tension between us, and I was sometimes embarrassed by his lack of career and financial success. But I lost a compass, however faulty I thought it was.

Dad served in the British army during World War II, including fighting the Japanese in Burma. But he never spoke of his war experiences or about other personal issues.

He finished an aircraft maintenance training program in Bristol and Cardiff, U.K., after the war. A couple of his Indian classmates achieved success upon returning to India.

One of them, who worked for Air India, was a smooth, ambitious Keralite. He pleased his bosses and rose rapidly to become a senior manager. He bought a three-bedroom apartment on Linking Road in Bandra, an upscale suburb, in the 1960s.

Another was Lal, a Punjabi, who started an engineering business in Mumbai. He visited Dad in his chauffeur-driven Impala car, which stood out amidst the small, boxy Indian-built Fiat, Ambassador and Standard cars. He invited us to his large apartment on Peddar Road, where he had a south Indian cook Chintamani make special north Indian rotis.

Dad was skilled at his work and believed in meritocracy. He did not play office politics and would have failed, if he tried, since he was blunt. He was not promoted at Air India and did not get sent for training to the Boeing plants near Seattle.

He did not seek a higher paying job at an airline in the Persian Gulf because he did not want to live as a third class citizen. He was good at investing in real estate and tried to broker the sale of a big plot of land to a major business.

Dad never complained and did not criticize others. He bought lottery tickets and believed in astrology, in his search for ways to get out of a stagnant career.

He went out to the front yard to chat with an astrologer who visited every few years. This astrologer dressed in white robes, had a long, full beard and scary, piercing eyes. He told Dad he would come to a major obstacle in his life which, if overcome, would lead to big success.

Dad would have found out that he got a major promotion, with a 20% raise in wages, on the day he died. He had passed an exam at Air India, which Mom had convinced him to take.

His anxiety over the astrologer's forecast, and if he would be selected for a promotion, may have been the trigger for his heart attack, compounding the heart problems he had from smoking.

A neighbor, Cherian Kolady, helped Mom with the months of paperwork required to collect Dad's pension and retirement benefits. Cherian was a quiet man, also a Keralite Christian, who worked at Air India. He spent Sunday afternoon cleaning and tinkering with his Fiat car. His children were in the same school as my siblings and me.

## Dealing with Bullies

Following Dad's death, I went to church daily and became an altar boy. I was nervous during Mass about when to ring the bell and bring the wine, especially with the head priest. He would shout at the altar boys for making errors in the midst of the church service. Some of the altar boys drank the wine found in the sacristy when the priests were not around.

I resumed playing cricket, following Aunt Philo's advice, with a team that played the official and expensive game with safety leg pads, gloves, a five-and-one-half ounce hard red ball and willow bats seasoned in linseed oil.

We played on a pitch in a large open field, where Mumbai University's Kalina campus was under construction. Earlier I had played cricket with tennis balls and cheap wooden bats, like most Indian boys.

I tried out for the school soccer team, wearing my older brother's boots, which were two sizes bigger for me. I was not a fast runner but was disappointed that the captain chose one of his friends over me.

In the 1990s, when living in Scarsdale, New York, I was one of the few dads who had played the game. So I got to coach teams in which my three kids played.

I gave up being an altar boy, finding that Catholicism did not answer questions about suffering, loss and injustice. I continued going to Mass and Catechism class on Sunday to see a girl I wanted to date but was nervous to approach. She closely resembled Ms. Annie, my fifth grade teacher.

The Catechism class was taught by Father Christopher, who later gave up his religious vows to get married. There were three other priests from the church who got married.

One of them was Father Nelson, in his 30s, six feet tall, fair, with a lean face and long wavy hair. He was intense, had a booming laugh, played the acoustic guitar and sang folk songs. He was very popular, especially among the high school girls and women teachers. In 1975, Nelson and I taught at Greenlawns School, and we became friends.

Father Christopher was in his late 30s, with glasses and clean shaven, like the other priests. He encouraged students to ask questions and argue, and it was a lively class. I asked questions and got into arguments to impress the girl. While she was not impressed, a couple of classmates taunted and pushed me, calling me an atheist.

In middle school, I had gotten punched for not letting bullies copy my answers during tests and exams. Mom told my brothers and me to deal with bullies on our own and not bring home any complaints. I once got a bully to scare a kid bigger than me. But soon the bully demanded I give him cash and gifts. I quickly learned to beware of riding a tiger.

One time a friend Keith gave a black eye to a bully who slapped me for ignoring him. I asked George Abraham to help. He asked Babloo Ghosh, who got a bodybuilder to warn the bully against harming Keith or me. The bodybuilder was the son of a church employee. Babloo became a doctor and Georgie, whom I have known since the second grade, a politician.

A few of the bullies in school ended up in local mafia gangs. One of them built his reputation by showing up at the school gates with a koyta, or sickle, used to cut grass. He threatened to attack a teacher for caning his cousin.

### Regaining Interest in School Studies

The qualification for admission to the merchant navy program was changed to a minimum 50% grade in the First Year College Science exams. I had to get good grades at the final 11th grade exams, especially in algebra, geometry, physics and chemistry, to get into a good science college.

But I fared badly in the tenth grade exams and was not allowed to take algebra and geometry in the 11th grade. Mom met Father Lobo, the head of the school, and convinced him to let me study algebra and geometry. She said I would take tuitions and improve my grades.

I took math tuitions from Mrs. Shenoy. She was a calm and patient teacher, who taught grades 7 to 11. After school, she tutored dozens of students. She charged Mom only half the regular monthly fees, Rs.25 or $3.

There were five bright, motivated classmates in my tuition group. We sat around the laminated dining room table at Mrs. Shenoy's home near where I lived. I quickly found I enjoyed solving problems in Euclidean Geometry and elementary Algebra.

My improving performance in math revived my interest in studies. I woke up at 5:00 a.m. and studied for two hours before going to school. After school, I finished my homework and studied from 2:00 p.m. till 5:00 p.m. and for about an hour at night.


My science teachers were men, recent migrants from Kerala, who taught while seeking better paying technical jobs at a big company. They were nice folk, and put in much effort, but were mediocre teachers. Also, their job was made difficult by having to teach a class with over 40 students.

I needed to improve my grades in physics and chemistry. I got free tutoring from Jose, a relative who taught at Bhavan's College in Andheri. He had a Master's in Physics from a university in Kerala.

Jose was a short muscular man, clean shaven, with curly hair and sharp features. He made his points with forceful emphasis softened by a smile. He moved back to Kerala after he retired, a dream of many Keralites, including Dad.


Beena David, the 11th grade English and home room teacher, organized tours of the Kwality ice cream and Coca Cola bottling plants. Students were given a free cup of vanilla ice-cream at Kwality. But, on the bus back to school, some were eating chocolate ice cream bars they had lifted from the factory.

I visited Ms. David with a couple of classmates. She lived with her mother in Pali Hill, Bandra, in a large house with a big yard. A few years later, her house was torn down and replaced with a multi-story luxury residential building.

In March 1971, I took the final 11$^{th}$ grade exam, the Secondary School Certificate.

### Campaigning for Indira Gandhi

After the exams, I campaigned for Prime Minister Indira Gandhi's Congress Party for the national parliamentary elections held later that month.

Indira Gandhi's government depended on the support of regional parties, due to a split in her Congress Party in 1969. She called the elections, a year ahead of schedule to try to benefit from a surge in nationalist pride. This arose from India's support for the revolting East Pakistani soldiers who sought independence for the region from Pakistan.

Gandhi's economic platform for the elections was "Garibi Hatao," get rid of poverty. This slogan, in some variation, has been used by every politician and political party in India since elections were first held in 1951.

I rode in an open Mahindra jeep, fitted with a loud speaker, one of the volunteers handing out flyers. The elderly owner of a local store, also in the jeep, asked voters to stamp the cow and calf symbol on the ballot and re-elect Gandhi's Congress party.

His store was the largest in Kalina. It sold rice, wheat and sugar, on behalf of the government's ration system, and school text books, Colgate toothpaste and Cadburys' chocolates. The store likely made its biggest profits from selling sugar.

Mrs. Gandhi's party was re-elected, winning 352 out of 518 seats. Her party got only 44% of the votes but won due to the splintering of the opposition votes.

In December, India and Pakistan fought their third war with Indian troops helping the revolting soldiers in East Pakistan establish an independent Bangladesh.

I was happy when I got my SSC results in June, securing 410 out of 700 marks - just missing a first class, or 60%. I got 81% in math though only 43% in physics and chemistry.

I applied to study science at St. Xavier's College but was rejected since the cut off for admission was 62%. A Jesuit priest and college official told Mom I could join the arts, or social sciences, program, which had a 55% cut off. I declined, though three years later, I switched to studying social sciences.

Today the chances of being admitted to the top colleges in Mumbai and other Indian cities are far lower. Nida Najar wrote about students who did not get into the top colleges in Delhi but were admitted to Dartmouth and the University of Chicago, in an article titled, "Squeezed Out in India, Students turn to U.S." in 2011 for *The New York Times*.

"Can't get into DU (Delhi University), can make it to the Ivies," she quotes the mother of a student going to Dartmouth.

The parents of the Indian student admitted to Dartmouth would have had to pay over $30,000 a year for tuition and room and board after getting $20,000 in funding from the college. In contrast, the total annual costs at the top colleges in Delhi is only $500, due to massive government subsidies.

Najar did not discuss the financial burden Indian middle class parents assume when they take loans to fund their children's education at U.S. and European colleges. Those studying computer science, engineering, math and the natural sciences may find high paying jobs that will help them repay the loans.

But the burden of education loans, especially for liberal and social science courses, is hurting even middle class Americans. As of January 2016, 3.6 million Americans were in default on school loans totaling $56 billion; not making a payment for over a year. Another three million got permission to halt making payments on $110 billion in loans due to factors like loss of jobs.

The burden on middle class Indians can only be higher since the loans for education in the U.S. are a far bigger multiple of annual income in India. Indian banks must face rising default rates on such loans, though there is little discussion of this in the media.

## Chapter 6

## CLOSE, BUT NO MEDICAL STUDIES

I enrolled in Wilson College, facing Chowpatty Beach in South Mumbai, eager to study at a college in the city. It was founded in 1832 by a Scottish missionary John Wilson and run by the Protestant Church of North India. It has stone buildings, archways and courtyards, a basketball court and, about a mile away, a field for cricket, soccer and hockey.

### Failing the Merchant Navy Exam

There were about 3,000 undergraduate students in the college, equally divided between the science and arts, or social science, programs. The students were mostly Maharashtrians and Gujaratis living nearby.

I wore bell bottoms, with wide belts, and colorful silk shirts with large flowers. I tried to grow my hair but, being curly, it just bunched up around my head.

I also wore cotton shirts, bought for Rs. 15, or $2, from street vendors in Mumbai's Fort area. The shirts, with fashionable collars and cuts, had no labels and were one third the price and of superior quality to those sold by major local brands. I later found out that they were donated by Americans and Europeans for

Bangladeshi refugees.

There were some good teachers, but I rarely spoke to them since there were 150 students in my class. I did not understand calculus, trigonometry and advanced algebra. I took tutoring in math and managed to get 50% in the first year final exams.

But I failed the exam for the merchant navy program. I was not upset since I was one of 800 selected for interviews for the officer training program at the National Defense Academy.

The selection was based on an exam, taken by about 15,000 sixteen and seventeen-year-old males. I had applied for the three-year Air Force pilot training program after reading an ad in *The Times of India*.

In June 1972, I took a train to an Air Force base in Mysore. I failed the Pilot Aptitude and Battery Tests, which measure hand-eye coordination. I was not surprised since I am clumsy and have no interest in mechanical gadgets.

I stayed an extra day to be interviewed for admission to the army officer's program. At the interview, I spoke emotionally about my Dad's death two years ago.

### A Hockey Goaltender

I was not selected to the army program. I continued at Wilson College, choosing zoology and botany, instead of math. This let me apply to medical colleges although I was not considering it.

I went to the first day of try outs for the college soccer team and realized I had no chance. Later I went for the try outs for the field hockey team. In the locker room, I heard the captain say he was looking for a goaltender. On the field, I said I wanted to be a goaltender even though I had rarely played hockey and never that position. I got into the team because nobody else who wanted to be the goaltender.

I was lucky not to have my face broken by the hard ball or a stick since I did not wear a protective face mask. Wilson's hockey team, as its other sports teams, lost most games, including 11-0 to Khalsa College, where I would later teach political science.

At Wilson I met Ashish Banerji, who had studied at Mayo College, a private residential school in Rajasthan. He was applying for admission to several medical colleges.

We joined a group of thirty student volunteers during the Diwali break in October. The group spent a week building a well at Balkanji Bari, a school for tribal Adivasi students in Dahanu, north of Mumbai.

At a nightly meeting of the volunteers, Professor K.K. Theckedath said he found out that the well was being dug for a landowner and not for the school. He was the faculty leader of the group, a mathematics teacher and secretary of the teachers union at the university.

The volunteers were upset at the news but decided to continue digging the well and investigate the ownership upon returning to Mumbai. The issue faded when we got back to college, and we never found out if the well was for the tribal students.

Mom got me an interview for an officers training program at the Shipping Corporation of India through a neighbor whose son she tutored. But I did not pursue her lead since I had lost interest in pursuing a merchant navy career.

I heard sailors repeat the same stories about their exciting adventures in various parts of the world. I realized they were the few high points, likely spiced up, while several months were spent staring at water. Also, I had no desire to own a Sony TV, JVC music system and Seiko watches after buying them cheaply at foreign duty free ports.

Years later I realized I would have been unable to work on a ship or on a fighter plane, assuming I had gotten into those career programs. I get nauseous even on ten-minute, winding bus trips.

## Slim Odds of Admission to Medical and Engineering Colleges

There were about 16,000 students in Mumbai University taking zoology and botany in the second year science program. Many of them hoped to apply to the four government-run medical colleges in Mumbai, which admitted 400 students each year.

The odds of admission to an engineering college were equally low for the 7,000 students studying mathematics in the second year at Mumbai University. There were two colleges in Mumbai University and fifteen government run colleges in other cities, which invited applicants from all over India. These engineering colleges were the second choice after the world renowned Indian Institutes of Technology.

Admission to the IITs was based on an entrance exam in math, physics and chemistry during the first year of college. About 2,000 students were selected to the five IITs in the early 1970's. Today there are sixteen IITs, which admit about 10,000 students - less than 2% of applicants.

Admission to the medical and engineering colleges at Mumbai University was based on grades in the second year final exams. They were one-shot essay based exams held in April, which could not be retaken to try to get better grades.

Students who wanted to get into medical or engineering

colleges, and whose parents had the money, spent over two hours each day at tutoring schools. The more expensive schools had good teachers, gave helpful study notes and held mock exams, so students could learn to pace their answers and figure out their weak areas.

The best of these was Agrawal's Classes, which had the most students admitted to medical and engineering colleges. It admitted students based on its own entrance exams and charged several thousand rupees in fees. In contrast the total annual fees at Wilson College was only Rs.450, or about $60, a year.

Some of the tutoring schools were rumored to sell exam questions. Stories about who had the questions and how much they charged spread rapidly on the night before the exams. Hundreds of students, parents and relatives wandered around Mumbai, late into the night, trying to buy the leaked questions.

Students with 63% or higher grades in the second year exams were admitted to the open seats at medical colleges in Mumbai University. Those from the scheduled castes and tribes got in with far lower grades. About 200 students, with grades just below 63%, got admitted to the two government-run dental colleges in Mumbai.

There were about 500 seats at medical colleges open to applicants from all over India. These were the top national colleges, all government-run, including the All India Institute of Medical Sciences (AIIMS) in Delhi and Wardha and the Armed Forces Medical College in Pune.

I took the multiple-choice based entrance exams for the national medical colleges, studying from work books borrowed from Ashish.

I was one of 120 selected for interviews, from 18,000 applicants, for the medical college at Wardha. But my grades, in the second year university final exam, were under 50%, the cut off for the second criteria for admissions to the national colleges.

Ashish was admitted to the Armed Forces College. He was one of the few students from Wilson to get into a medical or engineering college. The majority of those admitted from Mumbai University were from the top colleges Jai Hind, Ruia, St. Xavier's, SIES and Elphinstone.

Today there are AIIMS colleges in seven cities. They and the other national colleges admit about 2,000 students each year, an acceptance rate of less than 1%. In addition, about 48,000 students join other medical colleges, roughly equally divided between government run and private institutions, selected from about a million applicants.

The private medical and engineering colleges charge up to five million rupees, or $75,000, in admission fees plus annual tuition and other fees of over Rs. one million, or $15,000. So only the wealthy families can afford to send their children to these colleges. There are also some middle class students whose parents put up their apartments and family property as collateral to borrow huge education loans.

In contrast, there are no admission fees at government-run medical and engineering colleges, and the total annual fees are about Rs. 12,000, or $200. The competition for these seats is, hence, fierce and a major factor in Indian politics.

Several political parties organize protests and seek to win elections promising reservation of seats in professional colleges, and government jobs, to caste and linguistic groups.

The rise in the number of reserved seats has meant fewer seats for the majority of applicants who seek the open seats. Their odds of admission, to government-run engineering and medical colleges, is far below what the aggregate numbers suggest.

For instance, one hundred students are admitted each year to the renamed Mahatma Gandhi Institute of Medical Sciences at Wardha. But only 31 seats are open to applicants, irrespective of caste and regional background while 18 are reserved for backward castes, 12 for scheduled castes, 7 for tribes and the rest for other caste and regional categories.

### Contesting College Elections

I gained confidence in my academic abilities after I passed the medical college exam. I continued on for a degree in chemistry. The college also offered degrees in microbiology, physics, math, zoology and botany, paths to mostly teaching jobs in schools and colleges – assuming the grades were over 55%.

One of my chemistry teachers was James Barton, a Scottish missionary at the church, which ran the college and Wilson High School. He paced around the class, speaking in a booming voice, and was the most popular teacher. He was over six feet tall, muscular, with a trim beard and wore trousers and half sleeve shirts. He formed and led a Wilson rugby team that competed against teams from private clubs.

I gave up on field hockey and got into the college students council as secretary of the photography club. I never had a camera, did not know how to use one and I had taken few photographs. But I wanted to get into the council, and there was no one else interested in being secretary.

The club had a gallery and a dark room with equipment, chemicals and paper for developing films and printing black and white photographs. The club's previous secretary was a Kenyan of Indian origin. He was often in the darkroom with his girlfriend and with the door locked. He owned several cameras.

There was a Maharashtrian group competing against a non-Maharashtrian group for the key posts in the Students' Council. Kersey Katrak, a Parsi and the leader of the non-Maharashtrian group, ignored physical threats from a young Congress party official. He was a former Wilsonian and son of a police officer.

Kersey was elected chairman, and then had the Congress official banned from entering the college. I lost the election to become a secretary of the council, contesting as an independent.

In late 1973 there was a severe drought in Maharashtra due to a shortfall in monsoon rains. Madhav Chauhan, a student at the Institute of Science, started a fundraising campaign to help the drought-affected people. In 1994 he founded Pratham, a major education philanthropy in India.

I collected funds at Wilson, with help from some teachers. On Sunday mornings a group of students went on fund-raising drives. One morning we went to an area four blocks from Wilson College and the expensive apartment buildings facing the beach.

We entered tenement buildings of four floors, called chawls. There was a long, dark hallway with doors on both sides. The doors opened into a room with a row of beds, stacked three high, and tin luggage boxes on the floor. Men were sleeping or sitting on the beds.

The hot humid air smelled of sweat and tobacco. At the end of the hallway, there were a couple of toilets with a line of men waiting outside. There were also a couple of water taps, which supplied water for about four hours a day.

Groups of men stood outside the building entrances, in pajamas and shirts, smoking beedis. I asked a student where the men outside slept since the beds were occupied. He said they slept in the same beds after the current batch of occupants left for work. The men, working at textile mills operating in Central Mumbai, slept on the beds in three shifts. They worked in the city and sent money to support their families in the villages of Maharashtra.

I did not sleep well for the next several nights, seeing such poor living conditions for those who were employed. I was immune to seeing the beggars and the poor families who lived on the city's pavements and in huts made of cardboard boxes and jute bags along the railway tracks. I ignored them accepting Dad's opinion that they should find work.

The student volunteers from Wilson raised about Rs.20,000, or $3,000. The fundraising involved tasks like keeping track of the dates, places and cash raised, sending out and receiving receipts and filling out numerous forms at a bank and post office. I am thankful for this training in clerical tasks. But I found such repetitive task boring and did not want to work in a bank, corporate or government office.

### Early Steps to Journalism

I decided to switch to studying social sciences midway through the college year. I did not want to wear a white shirt and tie and visit doctors, selling drugs for Merck, Pfizer or Glaxo, the best career choice for a first class chemistry graduate.

I studied science and math in college because I wanted to be a merchant navy officer. I chose this career in middle school to try to match the goals of good students in my class who wanted to become doctors or engineers.

But, from an early age, I enjoyed reading about current affairs, history, politics and culture. There were no social science researchers or journalists in my family, among my parents' friends and among parents of my school mates.

I learnt about social science careers during the previous summer, while visiting Ashish in New Delhi. His brother Arup was studying for a Ph.D. in history at Jawaharlal Nehru University in the city.

Arup had a hipster beard and straight long hair which fell over his collar. He rode a motorcycle and had a leather bag slung across his shoulders. He dated a series of attractive women.

He chatted about his career plans for research and teaching at a university, preferably in Delhi, or working as a journalist. University jobs were attractive since they offered good wages as well as subsidized housing in most big cities.

In 1985 Arup stayed with me in New York for a few weeks, while he was doing research at Columbia University libraries.

In New Delhi, unlike in Mumbai, social science researchers were considered influential because of the political and policy debates dominating the discussion in the capital city.

Journalists were viewed as wielding power and connections and enjoying fame. The cartoonist R.K. Laxman, of *The Times of India*, and Khushwant Singh, editor of *The Illustrated Weekly of India*, were popular among India's English speaking elites.

I had to wait till the start of the next academic year to switch to studying social sciences. Worse, as per university rules, I had to start at the second year level, losing two of the three years I spent studying science in college.

While waiting to switch, I learned two valuable skills at Wilson College. I got into the habit of working at libraries. At first I could not focus on what I was reading from the textbooks while seated silently at a table with other students. I was used to studying with siblings chatting and the radio on.

For the first couple of weeks, at the college library, I read newspapers, *The Economist* and other magazines. Gradually I was able to focus on studying from the text books. Since then I have found working at libraries to be extremely productive.

I also began writing since friends said I wrote good letters. I had no plans of becoming a journalist. Also, less than a hundred English language journalists were hired each year by newspapers, magazines and news agencies in India. So the chances of finding work as a journalist were slim, even if I was interested.

My first published piece was a letter to the editor of *The Times of India* on college education. Mrs. Babu, my high school French teacher, told Mom she liked it. I was pleasantly surprised since I assumed nobody read such letters. Her husband, a lawyer, had lost an election for the legislature running Mumbai city as a candidate of a socialist party.

Next, imitating the style of *The Economist,* I wrote a two-page article for *The Wilsonian,* on the flaws of the Indian education system. S.K. Ookerjee, the editor of the annual college magazine, was a professor of philosophy. He was a graduate of the college, had a goatee and played the piano and organ in the college chapel.

I had corrections and additions after I handed in the article. I told Ookerjee I would give him a revised copy. He asked me for the changes and noted them on a pad. I wondered how he would remember since the magazine had dozens of articles and was over a hundred pages.

All my changes were in the article when the magazine was published. Some students and teachers said they liked my article.

In April I passed the third year final exam and thus got my three-quarter degree in chemistry.

## Chapter 7

## A TEACHER NICKNAMED

## CHARLIE CHAPLIN

In June 1974, I enrolled in the morning section at Elphinstone College, which ran from 6:30 a.m. to 9:00 a.m. I decided to study part-time for a degree in the social sciences and find a job since I had already been a full-time college student for three years. The college, founded in 1836, is located in a large building across from the Coomaraswamy Museum in South Mumbai.

The morning students were two distinct groups of mostly women, who did not socialize with each other. There were Catholics from Byculla, Dhobi Talao and the suburbs, working as stenographers and secretaries in private and public companies. They were hired for their command of English, the language of corporate business.

The second group were Maharashtrians from Girgaum and the distant suburbs, who worked as clerks in government offices and government-run banks and insurance companies.

The day college classes started after 9:00 a.m. Most students were from private English language high schools, whose fathers were senior managers in private and public sector companies, government officials, lawyers and businessmen. Elphinstone day and St. Xavier's were the top choices for arts and science colleges for Mumbai's English speaking elite.

Elphinstone was government-run, and so about twenty percent of the students in the day college were from Hindu castes who were admitted to reserved seats. They had far lower high school grades than students from the private schools and were from low- and middle-income families.

### A Culture Shock in Mumbai

When I first got to New York City in 1985, I was often asked if I experienced a culture shock. The Elphinstone day College was a culture shock.

Students from the private high schools socialized only with each other, ignoring those from the public schools with blunt snobbery. They were driven by chauffeurs in family or company cars and wore Levis and Wrangler jeans.

Many of them spoke of their summer trips to London, New York and Paris. Women smoked in the college cafeteria and yard. Until then, the women I had seen smoking in public were street sweepers and garbage collectors.

I applied for several clerical jobs advertised in *The Times of India*. But I got no response since I had no typing and stenography skills and no experience.

I interviewed for a sales job at an office supplies store located in a narrow, winding lane near the college. The owner apparently figured I might find it easy to sell to the office managers at private companies, many of whom were Catholics or South Indians like me. He said he would hire me for the job if I got a recommendation from a Congress party politician we both knew.

The politician had started his career working in an accounting office. He lived with his wife, kids and parents in a modest three-room apartment. He was a good speaker and got into politics by campaigning for Congress Party candidates.

He then got elected to the legislative body that runs Mumbai City. It issues licenses for real estate development and water and sewage connections and thus offers corrupt politicians and bureaucrats numerous ways to make money.

A few years after his election, the politician upgraded to a three-bedroom apartment, bought two-bedroom apartments for his three kids and a chauffeur drove him in an air conditioned Ambassador car. He continued to appear friendly, but I did not want to seek a favor.

I also did not want to earn commissions selling carbon typing paper, envelopes and staplers. The previous summer I sold a new brand of tooth powder, going door to door in the suburbs. The few buyers wanted to talk about their health and financial problems to a stranger. I gave up after a few days because I did not want to sell tooth powder that was more expensive and inferior to those sold by Colgate.

**Teaching Math in Middle School**

**A** few months later, Aunt Philo suggested I go to a non-profit placement agency run by a Catholic Church organization. The agency sent me to interview for the job of an assistant in the science laboratory at Greenlawns High School.

Asked to write an essay at the interview, I wrote about "Necessity is the Mother of Invention." Sara De Mello, the head of the school, wanted to know why I did not finish my science degree. I said I did not want to be a pharmaceutical drug salesman.

I got the job, and so the two extra years studying science in college were not a total waste. Ms. De Mello scheduled my work between 9:00 a.m. and 2:00 p.m. so that I could attend college in the morning.

The paint on the wooden window frames was the only thing green about the school campus on Bomanji Petit Road. The school functioned like a business while apparently run by a philanthropic foundation. The fees were several multiples higher than that at non-profit private schools in the city. The management appeared to have an ownership interest in the sale of uniforms, books and food at the cafeteria.

The school offered English language based education, in classes of about twenty students, leading in the tenth grade to a final school exam conducted by CISCE. This is a private school association in India, which was set up under British rule with help from Cambridge University.

The parents of the students at Greenlawns owned ultra-expensive apartments nearby. Most of them spoke little English and were unable to get their children into one of the elite non-profit private English language based schools.

Greenlawns did not have to comply with most government regulations since it was run for a private high school certification. It hired teachers like me with no formal qualifications. But there was no job security, medical insurance or pension benefits, unlike at government-aided and non-profit private schools. Yet the school attracted good teachers, some of whom stayed for decades.

My first monthly pay check was Rs.350, about $50. The headmaster Mr. Gomes handed me the check and said the school encouraged teachers to privately tutor students to supplement their low wages.

Most teachers tutored, earning several multiples of what teachers got paid in government-aided schools. The most notable was Mr. Ahmed, who taught Hindi. He joined Greenlawns after retiring from one of the non-profit private schools. He owned a two-bedroom apartment near the school, which cost over 200 times his gross annual wage from Greenlawns.

Raju helped me set up and clean the science laboratory. He was about five feet tall, with curly hair, and made funny remarks. He lived in the school building and functioned as the night security guard. He appeared to be the school management's extra pair of eyes and ears.

Each month Raju sent money to support his wife and kids living in a small town in Kerala. He did not have any technical or clerical skills and was, hence, unable to find a higher paying job in the Persian Gulf.

Besides running the lab, I taught math in third and fifth grades. I had a short mustache and students called out Charlie Chaplin when I walked by. I ignored them, recalling that I too had shouted out the nicknames of my school teachers.

A student at college told me I looked like a bad guy in a B grade South Indian film. Such stylized characters are scarier than in the typical Bollywood films. I preferred being called Chaplin.

### Gains from Choosing Fun Jobs

In June 1975, I was asked to teach math full-time in grades 5, 6 and 7, and my monthly salary was raised by 20%. I moved into student housing at the Telang Memorial Hostel for men from Elphinstone College on C Road near the Churchgate train station.

I took a six-week training course for teachers of modern mathematics at the Don Bosco high school in King Circle. The school, run by Salesian Roman Catholic priests, is attached to a church built of golden brown granite. The church has marble walls and floors, 23 stained glass panels and a twelve-foot gold plated statue of Mother Mary on its dome - all shipped from Italy in the late 1950s.

Charles De Souza replaced me in the science laboratory at Greenlawns. He is clean shaven, wears glasses and is modest. I have yet to meet anyone as generous as he. When I visited his apartment in Santa Cruz, across from the Sacred Heart Church, there were three or four people waiting. One wanted a loan, another came to borrow his guitar and a third wanted Charles to tutor his child for free. He met most such requests.

About once a month, after school ended and before tuitions began, I joined Charles, Nelson Pereira, a former priest at my school, and a few other men teachers for lunch at Allah Belli.

The Mughlai restaurant was run by Chillyas, Muslims with flowing beards and white caps, who formerly drove horse carriages. The food was tasty and moderately priced but not very hygienic.

I enjoyed teaching since I knew if students understood what I was explaining. I also found it challenging because I had to figure out better ways to explain topics that were not understood. I spent my work hours talking to students and preparing for classes and did not think about office politics. Teaching also motivated and recharged me for my own studies and reading.

For months before I got the school job, I worried if I would find a job I liked and if I should have taken up the office supplies sales job.

Since then, at several career crossroads, I based decisions on my interests and the best and most enjoyable long term use of my talents. My choices, while painful in the short term, have led me to bigger opportunities in all cases, except one.

## Opposing Indira Gandhi's Emergency Rule

I got to college around 7:00 a.m., attended one or two classes and then took a bus to my teaching job. I had some good teachers: Ms. Udwadia who taught English and Mr. Bengalee who taught Logic. They must have had a tough time since roughly half the students had a good command of English, the language of instruction, while the other half struggled with it.

I had prepared well but fared poorly in the second-year final exams. In addition to English and logic, the courses included economics, sociology, political science and history.

I had to choose what to study next. A degree in economics would have helped find jobs as officers in banks, insurance and other public and private companies and also to get into an MBA program. But I was not interested in pursuing these options and also would have to learn calculus to understand some of the economic theories.

I wanted to find answers about life, ethics and human nature and to "know myself," my influences and motivations and to understand others.

I expected to find the answers in philosophy, the source of early human knowledge. Also a new philosophical outlook helps bring about major changes in both people and societies. So I decided to study philosophy, without thinking about how it might help me find jobs.

On June 12, 1975, just before my philosophy classes began, the Allahabad High Court found Prime Minister Indira Gandhi guilty of corrupt practices in her 1971 election to Parliament. The court barred her from elective office for six years. She appealed to the Supreme Court to reverse the decision and continued in office.

On June 25, Indira Gandhi declared a State of Emergency, suspending civil rights and imposing press censorship. She claimed that a non-violent protest against corruption, led by Jayaprakash Narayan, was a threat to peace and the rule of law. Narayan had been a young leader in Mahatma Gandhi's non-violent struggle for India's freedom from British rule.

That night Narayan and thousands of leaders, from left and right opposition political parties, unions and groups, were arrested and jailed without judicial process. They included students, social workers and teachers.

Newspapers and magazines, owned mostly by families with business empires, were the only free media at that time since radio and TV were owned by the government. Censors sat in the offices of newspapers and magazines, deciding what could be published. The print media was banned from criticizing actions and policies of the government, ministers, the Congress Party and its leaders.

Two days later *The Times of India* carried a paid obituary in its classified section that read:

**O'CRACY, D.E.M.**, beloved husband of **T. Ruth**, loving Father of **L.I. Bertie**, brother of **Faith**, **Hope**, and **Justicia**, died on June 26.

This obituary was widely discussed in private conversations by students and others opposing the Emergency. I assumed it was the work of a brave Parsi, perhaps a lawyer, who ingeniously got around the censors. The young Congress Party leaders, who were studying at the college, boasted the person would be found soon and imprisoned.

It was only in 2014, while doing research for this book, that I discovered Ashok Mahadevan had placed the advertisement in the newspaper. At the time he placed the ad in 1975, he was an editor at *Readers' Digest India,* after having graduated from the

Columbia journalism school.

In a story he wrote for the monthly magazine, on the 35th anniversary of the Emergency in 2010, he says, "India became a dictatorship...People were too scared to jump queues at bus stops!" As a citizen, and more so a journalist, he was incensed that India was no longer a free country.

"Several newspapers - most notably *The Indian Express* and *The Statesman* - showed great courage during the Emergency, by refusing to print government handouts. Nevertheless on the whole, the Indian press "crawled" when it was only asked to "bend" by the censors, Ashok wrote.

One editor showing great courage was Krishna Raj of the *Economic & Political Weekly*, where I later worked. "The *EPW* kept alight the flame of democracy and a free press. It was Raj who...wriggled past the censor the first horrifying details of Sanjay Gandhi's forced sterilization plan - with young boys bribed with transistor radios to undergo vasectomies. In London, we thought it was back to the times of Pinochet's Chilean coup, and offered Raj and his family house room in exile," wrote Nigel and Tirril Harris in an obituary for *The Guardian*, the British newspaper, when Raj passed away in 2004 at age 66.

Another brave journalist was the cartoonist Abu Abraham of *The Indian Express*. The first frame of one of his cartoons showed an Indian politician, in a white kurta, pajama and Gandhi cap, making a speech. His words grow into a cloud above his head in the next frames. Then the words take on the shape of a bird. In the final frame, the bird lifts the politician in its beak.

On August 6, 1975, Prime Minister Gandhi got parliament to amend the electoral laws to overturn her conviction by the Allahabad court.

The dictatorial rule aroused wide opposition, especially

among students and the young. Stories circulated about prisoners being tortured and killed. The youth were also angry about the stories of injustice, favoritism and corruption – having to pay bribes for everything from getting a driver's license to securing a drinking water connection as well as admissions to medical and engineering colleges and government jobs.

I had taken part in student protests to oppose an increase in college fees and to seek an inquiry into allegations of corruption at Mumbai University. But I was focused on my education and finding a career and only mildly interested in politics.

During the State of Emergency, I felt suffocated and fearful. Civil liberty, as is said, is like the oxygen in the air. You take it for granted. You only realize its importance when it is taken away, like trying to breathe when there is no oxygen.

I took part in discussions on education, social and political reforms, in part through a student organization with links to a communist party. I was introduced to the group by Theckedath, a teacher at Wilson College.

Independent of the political group, Charles De Souza and I published *Change*. We distributed this free cyclostyled monthly of six pages, which summarized inspiring stories about struggles for democracy taking place in other countries. We avoided criticizing anything in India.

One day, amid the darkness of the emergency, I came across a quote from Rabindranath Tagore in *The Times of India*:

> "The worst form of bondage
> Is the bondage of dejection,
> Which keeps men hopelessly chained
> In loss of faith in themselves."

A Bengali writer, Tagore won the Nobel Prize for literature in 1913. One of his poems is the national anthem of India while another is that of Bangladesh.

## Lessons from Sanjoy Ghose

I was the only guy studying philosophy. For the eleven women in my class, philosophy offered the easiest way to get a degree with high grades and qualify for being promoted in their government and public sector jobs.

I read English translations of works by Aristotle, Plato and the other philosophers. But I gave up after a month, finding the reading too abstract.

At Elphinstone College I got into lots of arguments, over cups of tea, with several students. I get into arguments five minutes into the conversation upon meeting an Indian. Americans, who are with me, ask how long I had known the Indians. They are surprised when I say I met them for the first time.

Arguing is the favorite sport of Indians, after cricket. This is discussed by Amartya Sen, a Nobel Prize winner in economics, in a collection of essays "The Argumentative Indian - Writings on Indian History, Culture and Identity."

I was one of five editors publishing an unofficial student magazine. Almost all the articles were written by the editors. Mine were long theoretical pieces that nobody read.

I also wrote a 20-page article on the "Role of Intellectuals in Society," my first attempt at a long essay. It was a cut and paste of content from half a dozen articles and books. Mona Mehra, who was the sister of a fellow student Manoj and who worked at an ad agency, said the essay had no focus. Like others, she likely did not read past the first page. Such writing, though, helped later in my research and journalism work.

I learned much from observing other students. I also learned to find and work with those more talented than me, after being embarrassed by my performance in college debates, plays and other activities.

Sanjoy Ghose worked part-time as a researcher for the Center for Monitoring the Indian Economy, edited the college magazine, ran a literary club, led a group of students for week-long social service camps in tribal villages near Mumbai and was an award-winning debater.

He ran from task to task, rarely free to meet for "chai", or tea, the informal way of socializing among Indians. Yet he was calm and reflective, with an open and warm smile. He dressed in khadi, or hand spun, cotton kurtas and pyjamas and Kolhapuri leather slippers. While chatting, he would often update a written list of tasks to be done, people to phone and meet and articles and books to read.

Sanjoy was admitted to India's top ranked MBA program at the Indian Institute of Management, Ahmedabad. But he chose to study instead at the Institute of Rural Management in Gujarat, whose graduates were paid far lower. He ignored the opinion of Elphinstone day students, who viewed rural jobs as unglamorous.

He wanted to find ways to expand rural economic growth and help reduce poverty. He went on to study for a Master's in Agricultural Economics at Oxford University and in Public Health at Johns Hopkins University.

I last met Sanjoy in 1994 when he visited New York. He was working for a rural development and education trust which he had set up in Rajasthan.

He was eager to see the Trump Tower on Fifth Avenue, where the Bollywood star Amitabh Bachchan and another wealthy Indian family were said to own apartments.

In Central Park, as we ate sandwiches, he asked about the steps I took for my career changes and how I deal with former colleagues who say I sold out to work in fund management.

In July 1997, Sanjoy was discovered missing while leading a team of volunteers who were building embankments to prevent land erosion by the annual flooding of the Brahmaputra River.

News reports say Sanjoy was abducted and killed by local members of the United Liberation Front of Assam on behalf of contractors losing revenue due to the work of his group.

The Front organized protests and resorted to violence and terror, seeking more jobs and government contracts in the state for the Assamese. Its main target were Bengalis from the neighboring state of West Bengal, who held many middle class jobs in Assam.

It was a sad twist of fate that Sanjoy was a Bengali helping the Assamese poor by setting up health clinics and libraries and teaching them to earn an income by making bamboo products.

I have a handwritten letter from him, following his US visit, one of the few letters I have saved. He discusses efforts to get the Indian media to cover social work done by non-profit groups.

He wrote: "At this stage I must admit the scene looks quite bleak. Is it a crisis of values, or just a normal human characteristic to care less about others once one's own basic (and higher order) needs are fulfilled? It seems so out of fashion to talk about these things now."

I am reminded of Sanjoy every morning when I prepare a list of the tasks that need to get done.

### Finish an Exam to Get Good Grades

One evening, in early 1976, I chatted with Ajit Sanzgiri as we walked across Oval Maidan, ignoring the numerous cricket matches. He was a topper, a student ranked in the top 100 in major exams. He is the only one I know who got into the Indian Institute of Technology but decided not to join. He chose to study math at the Institute of Science.

I told Ajit that I knew the course content but did badly in essay-based final exams. "The most important thing is to finish the exam," he said. "Before starting, figure out how much time to allot to each answer. Then pace the answers and answer all questions. Do not spend extra time on an answer, since you will not finish the exam and hurt the overall grade."

I realized that during essay exams I spent extra time on a couple of answers I knew well or trying to answer questions I did not know. As a result, I answered only 8 out of 10 questions and got graded on a total of 80 instead of 100.

Also, nervous over not finishing, I answered the final couple of questions badly. Another problem was over-studying, getting little sleep the night before and being tense during an exam.

I prepared for the final exams with a focus on answering all the questions. I studied at the Mumbai University library, under the Rajabai clock tower, after I finished teaching and tutoring.

I made summaries covering the main topics in the courses on Western Philosophy, Indian Philosophy, Psychology and Logic. I read my notes and practiced answering questions that were asked repeatedly at previous exams.

In April, I answered all the questions in the first year philosophy final exams. I got 63%, a first class, and it was a high point of my academic pursuits.

# Chapter 8

# GRAY HAIR DURING INDIRA GANDHI'S EMERGENCY

At the start of the next academic year, I was elected secretary and head of the Morning College Students Association. I invited Durga Bhagwat to speak on Marathi literature since half the students in college were Maharashtrians.

I often chatted with Bhagwat at the Asiatic Society Library. The research library, housed in a large stone building with grand columns, was set up by the British in 1804. It has an original Italian manuscript of Dante's *Divine Comedy* and fragments of a begging bowl said to have been used by Buddha among its collections of rare books and artifacts.

A Sanskrit scholar and Marathi writer, Bhagwat had been the president of the Marathi Literary Conference. She was short, with sharp features, gray hair tied back neatly and horn-rimmed glasses. She was blunt, opinionated and a political conservative who opposed Indira Gandhi's State of Emergency Rule.

One morning in July 1976, Bhagwat spoke to over 300 students and teachers, packing the college hall. She began by discussing Marathi literature. She then said that the intellectuals who worked as censors and wrote articles, supporting the State of

Emergency, were cowards selling their soul to make dirty money. She criticized Indira Gandhi's dictatorship and the imprisonment, without trial, of thousands, including students and teachers.

After Bhagwat ended her speech, the audience hurriedly walked off in silence, with some fearing they could get into trouble at their government jobs for listening to the speech. I thanked Bhagwat and walked with her part of the way to the Asiatic library.

I feared that she, and possibly I, would soon be jailed. There was at least one policeman studying at the college. A few weeks earlier, he warned that he would have the police investigate me when I refused to answer questions about the newsletter *Change*.

I typed a brief report about this incident and tacked it onto a public bulletin board near the cafeteria, where students typically listed cultural and social events.

I barely slept and found gray streaks in my hair. In late August, the faculty adviser of the college students association asked me to attend a meeting. It was my task as secretary to set up such meetings, and so I suspected there was going to be a move to sack me from the position.

The adviser kept silent at the meeting while a student member said I had invited Bhagwat to attack Indira Gandhi's rule. I thought the member was a good person and had encouraged him to contest the college student elections. He wanted me to resign as secretary for misleading the association.

I figured my resignation would serve as proof that I invited the writer to speak for political reasons. I refused to resign. The meeting ended with the faculty adviser asking the student representative to speak to Bhagwat and report back.

I walked out of the meeting room and was happy to see Kersi Bathena, a morning college student, waiting to find out what happened. That afternoon, after finishing my teaching, I went to the Asiatic Library and told Bhagwat about the college meeting.

A few days later, on September 9, she was imprisoned

without trial.

Apparently the student did not talk to Bhagwat before her arrest, and so there was no follow-up meeting of the association. There were more streaks of gray in my hair.

One night in November, there was a police officer waiting for me in the lobby of the student residence hall. He said he had some questions and asked me to meet him.

He was the officer in charge of covering students for the intelligence wing of the Mumbai police. I had met him at student protests and would ask him about his kids and joke about his job.

I met him the next afternoon at his office at the city's police headquarters near St. Xavier's College. From his questions, I got a sense that someone had written to an official in New Delhi, likely Sanjay Gandhi, son of Indira Gandhi, about Bhagwat's speech.

It appeared the complainant was not a police spy but an Elphinstone College teacher, seeking to blame a rival colleague for permitting a speaker to criticize the government in a government-run college.

I feared I would be sent directly to jail. So I was relieved when the police officer said I was free to go after about three hours. I expected to be jailed soon but I did not hear from the police again. Perhaps the exchange of written correspondence between the Mumbai police and the Delhi political office took weeks.

On January 18, 1977, Prime Minister Gandhi announced parliamentary elections. She was confident of winning and lifted the State of Emergency. The fear was gradually reduced as Bhagwat and other political prisoners were set free, the print media began criticizing the government and protest meetings were held.

## Forced Sterilizations & Indira Gandhi's Defeat

During the roughly 18 months of Emergency rule, about 140,000 people were imprisoned without trial, including 33 members of parliament, other politicians, union leaders, teachers, journalists and students. Two students died during police torture in Kerala, the Amnesty International reported. Sixteen high court judges, who opposed Emergency rules, were transferred in punishment.

The loss of civil liberties led the middle class to oppose Indira Gandhi's Congress Party. The crowds at meetings of the opposition parties and civil liberties groups in Mumbai got bigger and bigger. This showed that the Congress Party would likely lose the elections in cities like Mumbai, Delhi and Kolkata.

But parliamentary elections in India are typically decided by voting in the Hindi-speaking northern states of Uttar Pradesh (UP) and Bihar. These states, with 85 and 54 seats respectively, accounted for over a quarter of the 542 seats in the Lok Sabha, the directly elected lower house of parliament. The newspapers and magazines reported that there were huge crowds at meetings of opposition parties in the Hindi belt. This was due to anger over the forced sterilization of men and women during the Emergency.

Sterilizations, mostly in the Hindi belt, was part of Sanjay Gandhi's strategy to tackle India's rising population growth. In November 1976, 700 policemen swooped on Uttawar village, in UP, and forcibly sterilized 180 people. In Muzaffarnagar, also in UP, police firing killed 43 people protesting forced sterilization.

Several hundred people died from botched sterilizations in UP and elsewhere. Such news was not reported in newspapers and magazines during the State of Emergency , except in *The Economic & Political Weekly*.

The wide public anger, and the fear of being imprisoned

again if Indira Gandhi got re-elected, pressured the leaders of the opposition parties to unite and form the Janata (People's) party. Its constituents ranged from left wing socialists to the right wing Hindu nationalist Bharatiya Jana Sangh.

The Janata Party and its allies agreed to back one candidate in each parliamentary seat against the Congress Party. In the previous two elections, the Congress Party won a majority only because of the splintering of the opposition votes among several rival candidates.

In March 1977, the Congress Party suffered its first defeat in parliamentary elections, with both Indira and Sanjay Gandhi failing to get elected. Votes were cast by 61% of the 321 million eligible citizens. The Janata Party won a majority 295 seats, with 41.3% of the votes. The party, and its allies, won all the seats in UP and Bihar and 39 of 40 seats in the other major Hindi state of Madhya Pradesh.

The Congress party got 34.5% of the votes and won 154 seats, mostly in the South with 41 seats in Andhra Pradesh and 26 in Karnataka. It also won 20 of 48 seats in Maharashtra, largely due to the support of the Maratha caste in the sugar-producing regions of the state.

Morarji Desai, 81, a leader of the Janata Party became the Prime Minister. Desai, who was a member of the Congress Party till 1969, lived until he was 99. He drank his own urine for good health and a long life, a therapy he discussed with Dan Rather on the CBS weekly TV show "60 Minutes."

In April 1977, I was part of a group of roughly a hundred students who entered the office of T.K. Tope, the Vice Chancellor and head of Mumbai University, and surrounded him with a human chain.

We wanted him and other senior university officials to

resign immediately. They reportedly raised the grades of certain students in the final exams which enabled them to gain entry into medical and engineering colleges. Their parents had either paid huge bribes or were senior politicians and government officials.

The action received wide press coverage, with *The Times of India* carrying it as a lead story on its front page. One of the students had his face in his hands in the photograph accompanying the story. Luckily, I covered my face before the photographer took the picture. I had taken the day off from teaching at school saying I was sick.

Tope and other senior officials were removed a few weeks later, one of the best achievements of my days in student politics.

There were news reports that colleges in Mumbai planned to stop offering morning and evening classes for social science degrees. They planned to use the classrooms for teaching higher fee-paying courses.

I helped Shiva Billava and Shekhar Amin organize a protest march of several hundred students from their night school and other such schools in South Mumbai. The protest likely stopped the plans, another good result of student politics.

The students worked mostly as busboys and waiters at Udupi restaurants during the day. They aspired to find a peon's job at a government-run bank or insurance company after finishing high school and passing competitive exams.

Many of them, once they found a job as a peon, took a series of exams to try to rise up the corporate hierarchy as clerks and officers.

One of the most satisfying jobs I have done is teaching a free class in logic for the second year exam, for morning and night students at Siddharth College. I taught three evenings a week, for a month before the final exams. The students, who had jobs during the day, were attentive, eager to learn and grateful.

## Philosophical Answers from Dostoevsky

The readings for my philosophy courses had improved my analytical and abstract reasoning. I was better able to recognize patterns and connections due my study of Aristotle's syllogisms, deductive inferences from a major and minor premise. I also realized it was okay to question established doctrines after reading about the skeptics.

I liked the Socratic method of asking a series of questions to understand an issue or expose flaws. The value of this process was reinforced by observing Krishna Raj, editor of the *Economic & Political Weekly*, where I worked from 1983 to 1985.

Anmol Vellani taught a course during my second year. He was "absolutely brilliant and awe inspiring as a lecturer," says Navroz Seervai, one of his day students.

Anmol was a recent graduate of Oxford University. He wore jeans and striped cotton shirts, with sleeves folded up to the elbow, and had his long hair combed back. He was generous of his time, directing a play put on by the morning college students.

He said his favorite philosopher was Ludwig Wittgenstein, who taught at Cambridge University in the 1930s and argued that philosophical problems should be studied in the context of the logic of a language. Anmol went on to do a Doctoral thesis on Wittgenstein at Cambridge.

One of the day college students was admired for getting a first class in the exams and his intellectual arguments. You felt honored if he spent a few minutes chatting with you in his quiet, measured tone.

One day I heard him tell a group of students that the first page of Albert Camus' *The Plague* was a great piece of writing, since it quickly and concisely defines the main character.

That afternoon, I started reading the book at the Asiatic Library, an English translation published by Penguin Classics. I read books and magazines there seated in a large leather arm chair by a huge window.

I found that the first page of the book describes the town and its citizens, not the main character. From then on, I was no longer nervous chatting with the intellectual and cared little about what he said.

I quickly finished the book, gripped by the story and insights - like how a person's traits of generosity or selfishness gets magnified during a tragedy. I read other books by Camus till I came upon *The Possessed*, his play based on Fyodor Dostoevsky's *The Devil*.

The characters were similar to many I came across in student politics and so I eagerly read *The Devil*. The story helped me understand the hidden hunger for power and control that fuels many of those pursuing noble ideals, as with the charismatic, selfish and manipulative Peter.

I read most of Dostoevsky's novels and short stories. I tried to figure out my desires and personality traits and their similarities and contrasts to those seen in my parents, siblings and other relatives after reading *The Brothers Karamazov*. When I come across a person acting like a fool, I am reminded of the elder Karamazov, a selfish and manipulative person.

Dostoevsky's works offered several insights: there is magic in small, everyday moments like watching a sunset; do not lie to yourself since then you cannot separate the truth within you or around you; humility gives you strength; if you respect yourself, then you will get respect from others; there are very few angels or evil folk, with most being driven by a mix of good and evil motives;

the nobler a person's goals, the baser the instinct that drives the person; and you can find out if someone is good by watching his laugh, not his silence or weeping.

The author's life - an epileptic, a radical youth facing death before a firing squad, years in Siberian exile, a gambling addict in debt and, in later life, a believer in Mother Russia - was as colorful and engrossing as any story he wrote.

## Don't Laugh too Much or you will Cry

I saw several "art" films, small budget productions by independent Indian and foreign directors. They were shown at theaters that had about 100 seats, while popular Hollywood and Bollywood films were screened at cinemas with over 2,000 seats.

In Krzysztof Zanussi's *Structure of Crystals*, a renowned scientist gives up a promising career in Warsaw to work in a remote region. He enjoys working with a crude weather vane, riding horses and playing with his wife and kids in the snow. Zanussi had degrees in philosophy and physics, before studying film, and so I assumed the film was autobiographical.

I later learned that Zanussi held senior positions in the state film hierarchy when the Communist Party ruled Poland. Senior officials in a Communist state crave power and fame, and so I wonder if Zanussi was being dishonest. I may find the film a naive ideological creation if I see it again.

I read a range of works, from novels by Nikolai Gogol, Emile Zola and Jean-Paul Sartre to plays by Bertolt Brecht and Samuel Beckett. Gogol's *Dead Souls*, with its dark humor, is one of my favorite stories. *The Overcoat*, another Gogol story about a mild-mannered civil servant, is one of the saddest I have read.

In the *Masterpiece*, Zola points out the character traits each facial feature represents, when he describes the future wife of the painter. I try to use the same technique to read a face, but find that I fail most times.

After reading the novel, I assumed Paul Cezanne was a failed artist when he was alive. But critics point out that Cezanne was a major success, and it was Zola who was a failure.

The works by great writers offer much wisdom, but my irrational fears continue. I get very nervous when things are going smoothly, especially over a long time.

Life is a tough struggle for most Indians. "Don't laugh too much or you will soon start crying," I was told by older relatives when I was very happy as a kid. This outlook is in contrast to the American goal of "pursuit of happiness."

"You only know you have been high when you are feeling low," sings the British artist Passenger, in his hit song *Let Her Go*. This is perhaps the best way to view events in life, since it's a mix of highs and lows.

I remind myself of what the French philosopher Voltaire said: the perfect is the enemy of the good. Yet I am nervous about errors before starting a project. I am more confident when I make errors at the start, so I can then proceed and finish.

I try to accept my mistakes, but I am often paralyzed by excessive self-criticism. I try to quickly overcome the impact of an error, but go on to make a second, sometimes worse, error.

Once Dilip Fernandez and I walked into a Greek diner in New York's Greenwich Village. I got into an argument with the owner, who did not let us sit at a booth by the window. I shouted it was not surprising his place was empty as we walked out. The owner rushed out after me, eager for a physical fight, and he was twice my size.

"When you get into an argument with such people, you stoop down to their level. You are never going to win that fight," Dilip said, while we had coffee at another diner. I agree with him, but have a tough time controlling my temper.

I should not be smiling when reading about easily avoidable problems created by celebrities, especially sports and film stars – like beating up fans of rival teams and waiters. I have gotten angry, shouted at bosses and lost jobs.

I once asked the employer of a former boss, why she hired him – while my former boss was standing with her. I hope to one day apologize to him.

I know Dilip from Mumbai, where he generously allowed me to stay at his apartment, while he worked as a reporter for *The Times of India* in Goa. He now lives with his wife Daphne and their two daughters outside London.

I have developed great respect for the British slogan during World War II: "Keep Calm and Carry On." And more so for a modified version: "Keep Calm and Win."

In college, I did not try to date many of the women I liked since their marriages would be arranged by their parents. I dated a few who were unlikely to have arranged marriages. All but one of them quickly lost interest, apparently because I had no career goals.

I did not continue dating the one who was interested in me because I did not know what I wanted. I tried to reconnect with her a few years later, after I began teaching at Khalsa College. But she was to soon marry a lucky man.

During one of our chats, when I gave an excuse for not doing a task, she said "a bad carpenter always blames his tools."

## Chapter 9

## FIVE RELIGIONS, FOUR CASTES &

## 22 LANGUAGES

I answered all questions during the second year final exams. I got a first class and was ranked 33rd out of roughly 10,000 students, who took the Bachelor of Arts exam at Mumbai University.

I realized the formal study of philosophy was a mistake. There was little chance of finding a teaching job with a Master's degree in philosophy. I chose to do a Master's in political science because of my interest in politics and since it offered better prospects for teaching jobs.

I was selected for a National Merit Scholarship, and the income from tutoring three kids covered my expenses. So I gave up my job at Greenlawns School and became a full-time student.

The day classes were held at the new campus of Mumbai University in Kalina, a ten-minute walk from the house where I grew up. In 1966, I had crawled through an opening in a tent and heard speeches by politicians and officials, when the construction of the campus began. In high school, I had also played cricket on a pitch on the campus.

Usha Mehta taught a course on Karl Marx, Mahatma Gandhi and other political theorists. She wore white khadi saris, which she first wore as a volunteer in Gandhi's Satyagraha, or nonviolent actions, that pressured the British rulers to quit India.

Mehta was a university official as head of the politics department. Yet, in private conversations, she said she was happy that student protests had led to the removal of the university's senior officials. She encouraged students to continue their protests against corruption and for a better education system.

## Top Civil Service and Management Jobs

I had no interest in a course in public administration, but it was a core requirement. The lectures by Professor Iyer were logical, concise and informative. He discussed the time and motion studies of Frederick Winslow Taylor, used to raise productivity at U.S. manufacturing plants in the early 20th century.

Iyer was reputed to set questions and grade answers for the English language based entrance exams used for selecting civil service officers. They are the backbone of the central government administration, originally set up by the British rulers.

The civil service was the best career path for students under 25, who earlier did not get into medical or engineering colleges. Today the exams are offered in both English and Hindi, and the civil service jobs are the top career choice for graduates educated in Hindi and the regional languages.

In 2014, 1490 officers were selected, including 362 for the elite foreign, administrative and police services, from over 450,000 candidates who took the exams. The 0.3% selection rate reflects the high unemployment among college graduates - about 15%.

College graduates are themselves a select group, despite the low cost of education. Only five percent of Indians have college degrees, while another one percent have technical certifications.

Since the 1970s, a management job is the top career choice for most graduates educated in English. There are over 2,500 MBA programs, but graduates of most of these colleges do not find jobs that can pay off their huge student loans.

There are roughly twenty good MBA programs, including at 13 government-run Indian Institutes of Management (IIM). In 2015, about 4,000 students, or 2%, were selected to the two-year MBA programs at the IIMs. There were over 200,000 applicants who took the English language based entrance exam.

An MBA from a top school starts with an annual salary of about $25,000, double that of a civil service officer. MBAs and civil service officers get free or cheap housing, the major benefit used by employers to attract good talent in India.

The Master's program offered students an option of writing papers for 60% of the grade; the remaining 40% was based on the final exam. I chose to take only the final exams, thinking I might not find time to write the papers since I was tutoring.

I tutored three days a week, walking up the hill off Napean Sea Road to the high rise buildings where the students lived. Cars whizzed by as I walked from the bus stop, and the few other pedestrians were mainly vendors.

The first exam was in political sociology. I spent ninety minutes on my first answer, twice what I should have. I had only ten minutes to answer the fourth and final question and wrote a two-page summary. I put myself in a statistical hole, greatly reducing my chances of getting a first class.

I answered all questions in the remaining three exams. I tried to speed up my answers by holding the pen in the air to avoid the friction of my wrist on the paper. I heard this was a technique used by successful candidates at the essay-based civil service exams.

But as expected, I got a low grade in the political sociology exam: 43% - in effect 43 out of 75 since I did not answer the fourth question. I did well in the other exams, getting 66% in public administration. But overall I averaged 55%, getting five percent short of a first class.

## Solving the Puzzle of Indian Elections

I wrote an 800-word opinion piece on the widening rift between the central and state governments in India over the sharing of tax revenues and expenditures. Regional parties who governed several states sought to expand their economic power while the Congress Party government in New Delhi rejected their demands. This tension took its most violent form in the state of Punjab, in 1984, with local leaders seeking an autonomous state for the Sikhs.

The piece was published in *The Free Press Journal*, my first article in a major publication and my first income as a journalist, Rs.75 or about $10. The Journal had the smallest circulation among English newspapers in Mumbai, after *The Times of India* and *The Indian Express*.

The gossip among journalists was that the Journal's newspaper business was losing money and that its owners made profits reselling the newsprint they bought at subsidized prices. The owners of major English and Indian language publications also earned income from renting out space in their buildings located in prime commercial areas. The land was given to them at low prices by the government.

During the second year, I took a course on Indian politics taught by Y.D. Phadke. He was tall, clean shaven, with glasses and wore half sleeve shirts and sandals. He spoke in a soft voice and grinned while discussing the characters, intrigues and ironies. He had sharp and clear insights into the complexities underlying the noise and heat of Indian politics.

The first piece of the electoral puzzle is religion. The major religion is Hinduism, the faith of three quarters of the 1.3 billion population including the tribals. The tribals, about a tenth of the population, also have their own animistic religions. About 180 million, or 14%, are Muslims, the second-highest number in a country, after Indonesia. Sikhs and Christians are each about 2%, and Buddhists about half a percent.

The Hindu votes are typically split based on caste. The Kshatriyas, or peasant and warrior caste, are the largest in numbers. They are the major beneficiaries of political power since the first elections in 1951 gave votes to all those over 21. The Vaishyas, or business castes, are few in number but very influential in politics and policy based on their control of much of the trade and business.

The Dalits or Scheduled Castes, the caste of laborers and artisans, is the second largest number of Hindus. They are mostly poor and less educated, like the Muslims. The leaders of the Dalits and Muslims were members of the Congress Party or aligned with it until the 1960s, enabling the party to rule the central and most state governments.

The Brahmans, the priestly caste, are highly educated but are small in numbers and, hence, have little political clout.

About 40% of the population speaks Hindi, and they live in Uttar Pradesh, Bihar, Madhya Pradesh and other northern states. The people in most of the 29 states have separate languages, scripts, culture, customs and food. Most states have local political parties championing linguistic-based interests.

Major languages include Bengali in West Bengal; Gujarati in Gujarat; Kannada in Karnataka; Malayalam in Kerala; Marathi in Maharashtra; Tamil in Tamil Nadu and Telugu in Andhra Pradesh and Telangana.

Political victory in state elections is determined by alliances among caste, religious and tribal parties and groups. At the national level, the contest is between the Congress Party and the Bharatiya Janata Party (BJP.) They form alliances with linguistic parties and groups, in addition to religious, caste and tribal alliances, to try to win parliamentary elections.

The current Prime Minister Narendra Modi is from the BJP, starting out in politics as a member of the Rashtriya Swayamsevak Sangh (RSS). The BJP is "ideologically captured and organizationally controlled by the RSS," writes Sudheendra Kulkarni, an adviser to the former BJP Prime Minister Atal Bihari Vajpayee, in *The Indian Express* in January 2016.

The RSS, Kulkarni continues, has always claimed that "Hindu Rashtra" (a nation of Hindus) and "Akhand Bharat" (an India unified with Pakistan and Bangladesh) are its core beliefs.

## A Pioneer in Online Journalism

In October 1978, I visited the office of the *Economic & Political Weekly*. It carries one or two page analytical reports on Indian and global issues, by leading journalists and academics. It also has three or four research articles on mostly Indian topics, with footnotes, and a couple of book reviews.

I chatted with the editor Krishna Raj, after an introduction from his deputy M.S. Prabhakara. Raj asked me to review a book *Party and Democracy in India* by S.N. Sadasivan, a professor at the Indian Institute of Public Administration and author of several books on Indian politics.

My roughly 1,000-word review said the book classified Indian political parties using a grid with ideology and party size as the two axes. The book ignored the caste and religious divisions crucial to understanding Indian elections. It had lots of data, but the analysis was superficial and wrong, like claiming that Prime Minister Indira Gandhi's Emergency Rule was a minor aberration.

Mukul Pandya, studying for an MA in economics, said he liked my review. I first met Mukul since we were both opposed to the Emergency Rule. He worked for *The Economic Times* in Mumbai after his MA. After migrating to the U.S., he wrote freelance stories for *The New York Times, The Wall Street Journal* and *The Economist*.

He is a pioneer in digital publishing and podcasting, as founding editor-in-chief of the Wharton School's online journal *Knowledge@Wharton* since 1999. It has three million subscribers globally, with editions in English, Chinese, Spanish, Portuguese and one for high schools. This is an affluent, educated, global readership much sought by publishers like *The Economist* and *The New York Times*.

Mukul is a prominent American journalist who did not go to journalism school. Also, he did not get a degree in the U.S., unusual for a successful Indian professional in the U.S.

Lucky for Wharton that Mukul is devoted to the goal of spreading free knowledge through an academic institution, following the example of his parents who taught at Mumbai University. His financial net worth would have been very substantial had he worked at a for-profit online publication.

I may be biased since Mukul has published my pieces in *Knowledge@Wharton*, including on investing in emerging markets and India's cricket success.

### Politics: the Best Career in India

I answered all questions at the second year final exams. I got over 60% in Phadke's course on Indian politics, but 51% in international politics, my least favorite course comprising of theories that did not explain any major global issues. I asked for a re-evaluation but my grade was left the same. I got 57% overall for the degree and was disappointed at missing a first class.

Several fellow students found jobs as officers, including in government-run banks and insurance companies and the civil service. These were good careers, with jobs for life, housing, health care coverage and pension plans. But I had no interest in working in a bureaucracy, given Dad's experience at Air India.

I continued tutoring three students and enrolled at the Government Law College for the three-year law degree from Mumbai University.

Many of the political leaders in India are lawyers. Young leaders, from across the political spectrum, were enrolled at the college. They wanted to win elections to the student government, impress senior party leaders and move up to contesting elections to the city, state and central legislatures.

Joining a major political party and winning elections is the best career path to wealth, fame and power in India, though the competition is fierce and at times physical.

The tactics to win college elections are similar to winning political elections: forming the right linguistic and caste alliances and splintering the votes of the opposition. Student leaders from the major political parties used muscle power to win elections in most colleges in Mumbai by threatening and assaulting rival candidates and forcing them to withdraw.

I supported some students in the law college elections. I then helped put together an alliance that won all the key posts of president and secretaries, defeating candidates of the Congress Party and other political groups. All the elected students officials, except Dilbur Parekh, ignored me after the elections were over.

Earlier, during my Master's studies, I realized that the goal of all politicians was the same: to win and retain power by any means possible. Many left and liberal politicians hid their pursuit of power behind a mask of noble ideals. The mask began to peel off after the State of Emergency was lifted.

Even if interested in political power, I realized I had little chance of success in Mumbai since I was a Christian and South Indian. The majority of voters in the city were Maharashtrians and Gujarati Hindus.

I took part in a mock court competition at the college. I got help from Navroz Seervai, whom I knew from Elphinstone College, and now a major lawyer in Mumbai. I did badly in knowledge of law and as a debater. I gave up on law and did not take the first year exams.

## Seeking an Escape from Mumbai

I was eager to live outside Mumbai for at least six months to figure out my career plans. I considered working at a hotel in a resort area like Goa. But I realized I would be exhausted from work and not have much free time to relax and reflect.

I searched for research institutes outside the city where I could pursue an M.Phil. or a Ph.D. I wanted to study economics to improve my chances of finding a career in teaching, research or journalism. But the major universities in India required an applicant to have a Master's in Economics.

Shakti Cherian, a research fellow in sociology at Mumbai University, told me about an M.Phil. in Applied Economics at the Centre for Development Studies (CDS) in Thiruvananthapuram,

Kerala. CDS focused on empirical study of economic issues, using a multi-disciplinary approach, and admitted students from non-economic backgrounds.

I wrote a six-page thesis proposal on the sugar cooperatives in Maharashtra as part of my application to CDS. The politics in the state were controlled by leaders of the sugar cooperatives, the sugar barons. They included most chief ministers, who head the state government, and the key central and state ministers. I would analyze the economics of the sugar cooperatives to understand the political power of the barons. I got help on my proposal from Shakti and Professor Phadke, one of my political science teachers.

During my interview for admission to CDS, I was asked if I could reason in the abstract, to be able to understand theoretical models in economics. I said my study of logic and philosophy required abstract thinking.

I stopped tutoring after the final exams in April 1980, hoping to get admitted to CDS or find a college teaching job. I applied to over a dozen jobs to teach political science at colleges in Mumbai University.

My Master's grade was above the 55% cutoff to qualify for such jobs, and I had three years of teaching experience. I got called to only two interviews and was rejected at the first.

I gave up on finding a teaching job since the new academic year was to begin in two weeks. I lay in bed with a flu at a fifth floor walkup apartment I shared with Ajit Sanzgiri and a couple of other graduate students.

Bibu Bose visited me and treated me to beer and dinner. The informal rule, with him and other good friends, was that we shared the cost of meals in proportion to one's income. He was a fellow student in political science, was elected to the Mumbai University Senate and worked at the government-run New India

Insurance Company, a property and casualty insurer.

A few days later, I got a letter asking me to attend an interview for teaching grades 11 and 12 at the Guru Nanak Khalsa College. In 1977, a new system of education was introduced in India, with 10 years of school, two years of junior college and three years for an undergraduate degree.

I wore a white shirt, dark maroon trousers and rubber slippers for the Khalsa interview. The college, run by a Sikh philanthropic institution and founded in 1937, is one of the few in Mumbai with a nice campus. It has a large rectangular building of three floors, with a columned entrance leading into a central courtyard with flowers and plants.

### Avoiding Physical Assaults

I joined some students from my Master's class outside the office of the Principal, or head, of the college. We chatted politely, while waiting to be interviewed for the same job.

I was nervous when I walked into the office of the Principal Raghuveer Singh. It was my last chance of finding a good teaching job. One of the interviewers was Usha Mehta, head of the political science department at Mumbai University.

In response to one of her questions, I said I wanted to teach because I like teaching and had taught for three years. The phone in the office rang, and Singh picked it up. He listened for a few minutes, said "I will look into it" and resumed my interview.

Two days later I met Singh again, after receiving a hand delivered letter inviting me to a second interview. He was over six feet tall, broad shouldered and stocky, with a gray beard and a turban required by his Sikh religion.

A man of few words, he was blunt but friendly. He said the phone call during my interview was from a former Khalsa student who told him not to hire me because I will create political trouble.

Singh said Professor Mehta defended me saying I was a good student and not a trouble maker. He said he got his first job, at a Khalsa college in Punjab, because the head of the college gave him a chance. He said he was giving me a chance but would watch me closely.

I recalled greeting a former student leader of Khalsa while waiting for the first interview. He was the one who likely phoned Singh. A year earlier he had joined in a student protest, seeking a delay in the start of Mumbai University's final exams.

After the protest ended, he told some students he was going to physically assault me because I agreed to a delay of three days instead of a week.

George Abraham said he told the Khalsa student that I was not to blame. The protest had to be called off since it rapidly got out of control. Over ten thousand students joined a rally at the Oval Maidan, seeking a cancellation of the final exams and automatic promotion to the next level.

Georgie was a student leader in college and head of the employees' union at Air India. He was elected to three five-year terms, representing a population of over 300,000 people, in the legislature that runs Mumbai City. Georgie reached a political plateau beyond which he could not rise being a Christian and South Indian.

There was another group of student leaders who wanted to assault me over the shorter delay in the exams. But Arun Ahire said he heard of their plans. Using colorful Bollywood language, he warned them against touching a single hair of mine.

He was tall, lean and muscular with a mustache and Bollywood idol Amitabh Bachchan-style-hair - long hair cropped like a helmet over his ears and his neck.

Arun was a popular student leader from Burhani College. He once filled the Bharatiya Vidya Bhavan hall in Chowpatty with over 1,000 screaming male youths dancing to Bollywood pop songs. The event was a fundraiser for an organization which helped unemployed youth find jobs.

He was interested in several social causes, and his energy and enthusiasm were infectious. But I did not agree with many of his political views, and we argued in Mumbai Hindi, Hindi mixed with Marathi and Gujarati words.

One evening we were having tea at an Irani restaurant when a waiter slapped a teenage busboy for spilling water. Arun got up, held the waiter by his collar, and told him he would be beaten if he hit the busboy again. Luckily this did not set off a physical fight since, being 5 feet 9 inches, 142 pounds and with no experience, I would have been of little help to Arun.

I visited Arun's apartment for a lunch prepared by his wife. Eating a meal at an Indian home shows respect for the host and can help build trust.

**Missing an Academic Year by Missing the Mail**

Khalsa hired me as a part-time teacher at Rs.10, or $1, per hour, though I had a full-time schedule. This was likely Singh's way of giving me a chance while protecting himself. I was fine with the position since it would make it easier to leave Khalsa if I got admitted to the Center for Development Studies.

I moved to the Khalsa College men's hostel, checking for mail at the post office every couple of days. In mid-August I assumed I was rejected by CDS since I did not get an admission letter. I could have phoned the center to find out, but feared I had done badly at the interview.

Singh gave me a full-time job, paying Rs.1200 or $120 per

month, along with medical and retirement benefits. In my teaching, I covered the right to liberty, free speech and judicial process, granted by the Indian Constitution; the reasons for the separation of powers of the executive, judiciary and administration; and the parliamentary system of government in India, with direct popular elections of members of the lower house, while those in the upper house were chosen by legislators from the states.

I mixed information from textbooks and real life examples and asked lots of questions, following the strategy of my good teachers. About a third of the roughly 80 students, mostly boys, skipped my class.

Those who stayed in class were a keen group of students, mostly Gujaratis and Maharashtrians and some Christians.

A teacher's seniority at the college was indicated by the size of storage boxes. As a new teacher, I had no place to put my books and papers in the teachers' common room. This was a large room on the third floor with comfortable chairs where teachers chatted, ate and worked. The storage space improved from a small wooden locker to a 4 feet by 3 feet Godrej steel cabinet as teachers rose to become the heads of departments.

I had several friends visit me at Khalsa because of the idlis and dosas at the South Indian restaurants in King Circle and the tandoori fish and chicken at the Punjabi restaurants in Koliwada.

The South Indian food was cooked and served by Tamils wearing white dhotis and shirts. They had lines of white paste on their forehead, put on while performing Brahman religious rituals.

The food was so authentic in its spiciness that some friends did not like it. They were used to similar dishes at Mumbai Udupi restaurants, fast-food style places owned by Shettys from Karnataka. They modify the Tamil food to suit the tastes of the large Gujarati population in Mumbai, who eat out often and prefer their food to be slightly sweet.

## A Cradle of Field Hockey, not Cricket

One weekend I visited Matheran, a less humid town in the hills about fifty miles from Mumbai. I got up early, walked for a few minutes and then sat on a small rock. I was wondering about what I would like to do next, while holding my head in my hands and looking down.

I heard a gravelly but gentle voice asking in Marathi, "Little boy, is everything OK?" I looked up and saw a thin, bent woman, with a sunburned, wrinkled face, in a cheap green cotton sari. I said everything was fine and quickly stood up, embarrassed and assuming she was a beggar. I was more embarrassed when she did not ask for money and went on her way to the bazaar.

My room at the hostel overlooked a field where Khalsa's hockey and soccer teams practiced. I watched the games, especially of the hockey teams, since they included my students.

The college is one of the few in India to focus on sports other than cricket. Its students consistently win major university and national athletics and sports competitions.

Jaswant Singh Grewal, the athletics director, was on the field at 7 am and left around 7 pm, traveling over an hour each way from his apartment in Borivali. His students went on to represent India at Olympic and world competitions.

I wrote a story on Grewal for *The Free Press Journal*. He chose athletes based on good work habits, team effort and a desire to win, in addition to talent. He spoke softly and did not shout at the students for making mistakes. He did not want to head sports and athletic associations, which offered lucrative foreign trips to meetings and conferences.

Grewal shyly said thanks and went back to coaching when I

gave him a copy of the full page story. I also gave a copy to Singh, the head of the college.

Grewal started at Khalsa in 1964 and retired in 2000. While India has great coaches like Grewal, it has done poorly at world athletic and sports competitions. In the 2012 London Olympics, for instance, it did not win any gold medals and got only two silver and four bronze medals.

India has done relatively well in cricket, winning the one-day World Cup in 2011. I watched this win live on the TV screens at an Indian restaurant in New York.

Indians, and Indian migrants, are the largest source of revenues for cricket, the most popular sport in India. Leading Indian cricketers make tens of millions of dollars each year. So the game attracts the most talented young athletes though the chances of being selected to the 16-member Indian cricket team are tiny.

The financial rewards from other sports and athletics are minor, compared to finding a good job. So Indian parents pressure children, who are talented in sports, to focus on academic studies.

Being a golfer, I keenly followed Anirban Lahiri's progress at the 2015 PGA Championship. Lahiri finished fifth, the best performance by an Indian in a major tournament. This will likely encourage more young Indians to take up golf.

I learned to play golf by practicing and playing at the public courses in Westchester, NY, using Tiger Woods' *How I Play Golf.*

### The Danger of Riding a Tiger

One afternoon, as I left the Khalsa campus, I passed a tall man with a flowing black beard, wearing the white kurta of a Sikh religious leader. He was flanked by two Sikh bodyguards with semi-automatic rifles slung over their shoulders. He was Jarnail Singh Bhindranwale, leader of a populist effort demanding greater autonomy for Sikhs in the state of Punjab.

The journalist Kuldip Nayar writes that Bhindranwale was initially funded and backed by Indira Gandhi's Congress Party. The Congress sought to groom a leader who could split the Sikh votes and reduce the popularity of the Akali Dal party in Punjab. An alliance, led by the Dal, had won the election in the state in 1977. Krishna Raj, editor of the *Economic & Political Weekly* and others, commented that it was risky of Gandhi to ride a tiger.

Bhindranwale soon demanded a separate Khalistan or land of the Sikhs. His armed followers took over the Golden Temple in Amritsar, Sikhism's holiest shrine. In June 1984, Indira Gandhi ordered the army to clear out the temple. Bhindranwale and over 600 others, including pilgrims, were killed.

Sikhs were angry at Gandhi over the killings and the destruction of their holy site. She was shot dead in her Prime Ministerial residence by one of her Sikh bodyguards, on October 31, 1984. Then, for several days, Hindu mobs attacked Sikhs in Delhi and elsewhere killing over 3,000 Sikhs.

In June 1985, an Air India Boeing jumbo jet, on its way from Montreal to New Delhi, blew up over the Atlantic Ocean killing all 329 on board. Canadian police reportedly say the plane was destroyed by Sikh extremists, though the investigation is still ongoing thirty years later.

Sangeeta Ghatge, a day student from Elphinstone College who I had met a few times, was a flight attendant on the plane.

## Chapter 10

## THE POWER OF SUGAR BARONS

Shakti Cherian, who had moved back to New Delhi, read one of my articles. She wrote asking why I did not join the Centre for Development Studies (CDS). I replied that I did not know I had been admitted. I wrote to the Director of CDS saying I did not get the admission letter and asked to be re-admitted to the next class.

This time I got the admission letter. I thanked Raghuveer Singh, head of Khalsa College, for giving me a chance. I named my son Niall, in part after Singh, modifying Nihal which means brave in Gurmukhi, the language of the Sikhs. Niall may have had a different name if I had called CDS to find out about my admission when I first applied.

One major regret at Khalsa was not attending the funeral of a student who died of an asthma attack. I can still recall her face, with dark circles around her eyes and hair tied back. I wrote a short story about my regret, a couple of years later, which was rejected by several publications.

### The Joy of Indian Train Journeys

I took a train to Thiruvananthapuram, the capital of the state of Kerala, where CDS is located. My six train journeys to and from

CDS, each over two nights and three days, revived and added fond memories. I had made this journey several times to visit Dad's relatives, with my parents and siblings, during school holidays.

Kerala is one of the most beautiful states in India, with beaches fringed by coconut palms, backwaters and canals flowing past rice fields, mango, jackfruit and cashew trees and hills covered with tea, cardamom and rubber estates. It is a major tourist attraction, especially for yoga devotees and for those seeking Ayurveda medical treatments.

The state has a 92% literacy rate, very good high school and college graduation rates, and the lowest poverty level in India, of around ten percent.

I slept on the top bunk of a Second Class sleeper carriage, for most of the journey, relaxed by the swaying train. In 1974, Indira Gandhi's government abolished Third Class carriages, inherited from the British, with much publicity about promoting social equality. The three class distinctions on trains, though, still remain with air-conditioned, First and Second Class carriages.

On the way south to CDS, I thought about what I need to finish during the next semester. On the train to Mumbai, I reflected on my work at CDS, tasks to do in Mumbai and about my next career move.

I eagerly awaited eating the local foods at the train stations: the karvanda, or berries, and chikkis, or peanut brittle, at Lonavala; the vegetarian thalis in Cuddapah; and the idlis, vadas, dosas and coffee in Coimbatore.

I reached CDS the day before classes began. The ten-acre campus, located in a southern suburb of Thiruvananthapuram, is on a hill covered with trees and flowering plants. It has red brick buildings dominated by a tower housing the library.

The legal upper age limit for banking, insurance, public

sector and government jobs in India was 25 for the unreserved seats. So for me, with a Masters' degree and over 25, teaching at a college was the last option for a good job. But getting such a job was not easy, as I found.

So the faculty and senior students assumed I did not show up the previous year because I wanted to hold onto the teaching job at Khalsa College. Some asked if I got leave without pay to study for an M.Phil. They did not believe my story of missing mail.

CDS did not charge students a tuition fee. Also, the fifteen M.Phil. students got a monthly fellowship of Rs.500, about $50, for the 16-month program and Rs.1500, $150, to cover travel and supplies for work on the thesis. The fellowship more than covered the room rent of Rs.25, $2.50, and the cost of meals, since both were heavily subsidized.

Government grants provided the funds for building and maintaining the campus, the wages for the faculty and staff, student fellowships and for buying books and journals at CDS and other research institutes in India.

### A British Architect's Exposed Brick Buildings

The research center was founded by K.N. Raj in 1971. He was an economic adviser to several Indian Prime Ministers, including the first Jawaharlal Nehru. He was also a member of the Planning Commission, which prepared India's early Five Year Economic Plans. He held a Ph.D. from the London School of Economics.

Raj taught an introductory course on national accounts. He spoke about the huge savings of the middle class in India. This is typically held in gold and low interest-bearing bank accounts. He said this savings ought to be tapped for investments to fund India's economic growth.

One day, following a discussion after class, Raj gave me a book. The author argued, with detailed empirical citations, that the French Revolution of 1789 was not a class struggle as portrayed by leftist intellectuals. It was the culmination of protests over taxes, food shortages and other grievances of the citizens. I do not recall the author and title of the book, and my efforts to find these have been unsuccessful since Raj passed away in 2010.

The first semester ran from September to December and the second from January to May. There were four courses per semester and, to my relief, no exams. Students were graded on two term papers each semester and the thesis.

I understood the cost plus methods for pricing goods for a term paper for Sudipto Mundle, who taught macroeconomics. But I could not figure out how to link theories of supply and demand to the macro theories of the economist Michal Kalecki.

At the campus I spent most of my waking hours in my second-floor room reading and writing. After the first couple of weeks, I was able to recognize the sound of my neighbor Rajaram Dasgupta's footsteps on the corridor outside my room. He was a research fellow and an ideal neighbor since the only noise I heard from him were his footsteps.

I found distractions from the monotony of being in the same spare, comfortable room, for two or more weeks. The walls showed a variety of patterns due to the uneven outlines of bricks, covered in white paint, in contrast to flat cement walls.

A concrete slab, set in an alcove in the center of the room, served as a work desk. Looking left, while seated at the desk, I saw the tower of the library, through a window. On the right, I saw trees through a glass wall. The door in this wall opened on to a small terrace with a bench, which faced a courtyard with trees, flowering plants and birds.

Similar elements of nice views, light and shadows, blending of the buildings with the hill and cooling air flow were evident all over the campus. I came to appreciate good architecture, which the architect Laurie Baker said was about common sense.

Baker's construction costs were half that of the concrete buildings common in India since he used less cement. He built over 2,000 buildings in Kerala, including private homes for senior CDS faculty, churches, schools, orphanages, earthquake and tsunami-resistant houses, government buildings, tourist resorts, a film studio and a museum.

Baker, who was British, was also a cartoonist and artist. He served as an anesthetist and nurse in the British army during World War II. He lived for four years in a remote area of China taking care of lepers.

He met Mahatma Gandhi and moved to India, working as an architect for a philanthropy which built homes for lepers in the foothills of the Himalayas. He moved to Kerala, married a Keralite and was an influential architect.

### Lesson from a B Grade in a Term Paper

A course in finance was taught by I.S. Gulati. He had retired recently from the CDS faculty. He had a trim gray beard and wavy hair down to his shirt collar.

Gulati's family fled Pakistan during the partition of India in 1947. He commuted to his first job, as an economist at the Indian Planning Commission, from a tarpaulin covered home in a refugee camp in Delhi. He got his Ph.D. from the London School of Economics, was an adviser on taxation and finances to the Kerala government and worked on a project with Nicholas Kaldor, a Nobel Prize-winning economist.

I asked Gulati if he was happy with his work as an economist. He said he was satisfied. But if he were to do it again, he would conduct research in the natural sciences since a discovery is universally valid. In economics and other social sciences, the same data and facts can be used by researchers and politicians to support widely differing, subjective conclusions.

I wrote my second term paper on India's balance of payments for Gulati's course, despite being told by senior students that he rarely gave good grades. Gulati asked me to read the chapters on balance of payments in Paul Samuelson's book *Economics*, prepare tables showing foreign trade and payment data and analyze the major factors.

I spent six weeks copying the data of the past decade onto large sheets of graph paper from books of official statistics. I left myself only ten days to read and analyze the major issues and write my paper.

The major exports were gem and jewelry, mainly small diamonds polished in Surat, iron ore and sugar, in years of surplus production. In the 1970s, unlike today, the information technology industry was small in India and so there was no software exports and no outsourcing revenues. The key imports were crude oil and raw diamonds brought in for polishing and re-exports by local merchants from De Beers, the global diamond monopoly.

Gulati said I had done a good job of collecting the data, but there was little analysis and no new insights in my paper. I was disappointed with his B grade, the lowest I got at CDS. But I learnt a valuable lesson to find and analyze the key elements.

India had a big and growing deficit on its current account, since imports exceeded exports. This gap was filled by savings sent home by Indian migrants working in the Persian Gulf and by capital inflows, mostly loans taken on by the government from the International Monetary Fund (IMF).

Gulati and other Indian economists warned that the growing deficit would lead to debt repayment issues, weaken the rupee, push inflation higher and cause social and political unrest. Brazil, Argentina and other Latin American countries had faced similar problems in the 1970s.

In 1991, India's foreign currency reserves could buy only a few months of imports. This pushed the country to the edge of bankruptcy and forced it to borrow from the IMF by pledging its gold holdings.

The IMF required the Indian government to reduce import duties, from over 110% to under 40% for some goods, permit foreign investments in more areas and allow private companies to operate in the insurance and telecommunications business, which until then were reserved for government-run companies.

These policy changes, which officials and some economists refer to as the exciting start of economic liberalization, have since continued haltingly.

Meanwhile, the Indian rupee has fallen against the major currencies. In 1991, a U.S. dollar bought about eighteen rupees. In early 2016 it fell to Rs.69 to the U.S. dollar, near the level it hit during the summer of 2013.

The fate of the rupee is tied to crude oil prices since India depends on imports for 80% of its supplies, I wrote in a story for *Knowledge@Wharton* in 2013. Financial markets were suddenly spooked by India's annual foreign trade deficit and the rupee fell by 30% during the summer of 2013. The deficit doubled over the previous decade to $196 billion, largely due to a five-fold rise in the cost of oil imports.

## Appeal of Bollywood Films

At CDS I woke up at 7:00 am and went down to the cafeteria to get tea. The cook Thankappan spoke some Hindi, having worked in the Indian army. Manian, his assistant, spoke only Malayalam which I do not know. I spoke to him using single words, "chai", "milk" and "sugar," and used sign language. He would laugh.

I sipped my tea seated on the steps at the back entrance to the dining room, reflecting on work I had to do and looking for parrots and kingfishers.

I liked the tea brewed strong, with milk and sugar. I drank eight to ten large glasses each day, including four in the morning. Later, on returning to Mumbai, I stopped drinking tea since the numerous cups dulled my appetite. I felt drowsy for about a week from the caffeine withdrawal.

Life on the campus, while comfortable and intellectually stimulating, was one of isolation since I grew up amid the various distractions of a big city in Mumbai.

I relaxed by listening to the greatest hits albums of Air Supply, America, Bread, Jim Croce and John Denver on a small Panasonic cassette player borrowed from Charles De Souza.

I went to see movies about twice a month with some fellow students. After the movies, we argued about films, philosophy, literature, careers and life, at restaurants serving arrack.

This home-made brew, distilled from fermented rice and other ingredients, was banned in 1996 after several people lost their eyesight and some their lives, after drinking adulterated versions.

A couple of film societies in the city screened films by non-Hollywood directors like Vittorio De Sica, Ingmar Bergman and Francois Truffaut. De Sica's *Bicycle Thieves* is one of my favorite films, along with Francis Ford Coppola's *Godfather 2*.

We did not see any morning shows of Malayalam films, popular among male college students. The theater owners illegally mixed in a few minutes of pornography with such screenings.

Most of the films we saw were Bollywood hits like *Kaalia* and *Namak Halal*, with Amitabh Bachchan playing an angry young man. Bollywood films, about two and half to three hours long, offer a simulated experience of major human emotions in a blunt, intense manner: bonds of family and friendship, celebration and fun via songs and dance, love, lust, humor, sadness, anger, betrayal, enmity, revenge, violence, rich versus poor and a happy ending of good triumphing over evil.

A few months before I got to CDS, I interviewed Vijay Tendulkar about violence and Bollywood films for *The Business Standard*. He was a social scientist who wrote plays and film scripts in Marathi and Hindi. He was awarded a Nehru fellowship to study violence in Indian society.

He said the millions of poor rural migrants, in cities like Mumbai, live like insects in slums and on the streets. Seeing the violence of popular good guys beating up bad guys in Bollywood films is the major release for their desire to fight suppression, compulsion and injustice.

Many of Tendulkar's twenty seven plays in Marathi and scripts for Marathi and Hindi movies explore violence in different forms: family, sexual, communal and political. His famous play *Ghasiram Kotwal (Ghasiram the policeman)*, a musical set in 18th century Pune, is a satire on the rise of the right wing Shiv Sena political party in Mumbai in the 1960s and its use of violence. The play has been performed over 6,000 times.

The outbursts of communal, caste and urban violence was

due to the persistence of feudalism, forced urbanization and mass poverty. Mahatma Gandhi's goal of "Ahimsa", or nonviolence, was utopian and an unattainable ideal. Men like Gandhi, Tendulkar said, "are strong men of very strong will and a large amount of ruthlessness. In their case, the violent urge, common to man, is molded into something constructive."

## Literacy and Healthcare in India

During the second semester, A. Vaidhyanathan, or Vaidhy, taught a course on Indian economics. He had worked at the Planning Commission in India and for the World Bank after a Ph.D. from Cornell University.

Vaidhy stressed the importance of analyzing data to arrive at conclusions, instead of manipulating data to support a thesis. He said the census and surveys of government departments were often two or more years old and the sample sizes too small. Yet, he said, the data gave useful insights and was better than having no data.

There has been very slow improvement in poverty, literacy and healthcare and a wide gap remains between the bottom and upper income levels. Roughly thirty percent of Indians are poor, by the World Bank's definition of people living on less than $1.25 per day. Eighty percent live on less than $2.50 a day and 95% on less than five dollars a day.

About a third of Indians are illiterate and the number is far higher - if the definition includes simple two-digit subtraction. In health care, two thirds of the population live in rural areas but are served by only a sixth of the country's health care resources.

"India is the epicenter of global malnutrition: 39 percent of Indian children are stunted from poor nutrition according to government figures (other estimates are higher)" writes Nicholas Kristof in *The New York Times* in 2015. Stunting of children is worse in India than in poorer countries like Burkina Faso, Haiti, Afghanistan and Bangladesh.

One theory explaining the stunting, Kristof notes, is that about half of Indians defecate outside without using toilets, resulting in children picking up parasites and chronic infections that impair the ability of the intestines to absorb nutrients.

In early 2016, the government began a campaign of giving de-worming tablets to about 270 million children in an effort to counter infections.

At the other end of the income level, about 137,000 households, each with a net worth of about $4 million or higher, owned about $2 trillion in assets, according to a 2015 study "Top of the Pyramid" by the Indian investment bank Kotak Mahindra.

These consumers, a small fraction of the population, are aggressively sought by Burberry, Louis Vuitton, Mercedes Benz and other global luxury brands.

Many economists expected growth in India to be much faster than in China after major policy changes were introduced in 1991. But India's growth has been less than half that of China's. Its share of world trade in goods and services has grown roughly four fold to 2.2% while that of China has risen ten-fold to 10.1%. The average Indian's wage of $1,500 per year is less than a quarter of the $6,800 wage of a Chinese.

## "Socialism" Protects Business Groups

The slow progress in India is due to its "continuing socialist legacy," say many economists. They blame the policies of Prime

Minister Jawaharlal Nehru in the 1950s, who is said to have been influenced by the Fabian Socialists of Great Britain.

There are restrictions on setting up a new business and bureaucratic hurdles like securing numerous licenses. Also, new companies have limited access to capital, unless they are backed by one of the major Indian business groups or big foreign companies and investors.

Overcoming these obstacles takes years, even decades, preventing most new competitors from entering a business. The policies hence serve as barriers that protect existing business owners from new competitors.

This is acknowledged in "Too good to fail", an article about the Tata Group by Ann Graham in *Strategy+Business*. "Before the 1990s, when Indian businesses were protected from outside competition but also limited by tight government controls, Tata's domestic expansion and diversification positioned the group as one of the two or three largest companies in India," Graham writes.

The article was published in 2010 by the consulting firm Booz Allen and is posted on Tata's website. Tata businesses range from salt and tea to steel and cars.

Setting up a new business became easier in the early 1990's, due to the IMF-imposed policies. But this change benefitted major multinational corporations and hurt Indian companies.

As Graham writes, the foreign expansion for the Tata's began in 1992 "one year after the Indian government lifted foreign investment and exchange controls and eliminated many restrictions on outside companies. Suddenly, multinationals such as Sony, Philips, Ford, and Toyota entered India, exposing the quality problems of many local companies and using their marketing prowess to outpace popular domestic players like Tata."

There are a few examples of major, politically connected groups expanding into new business areas dominated by a rival group in India. But the implicit pact among major groups seems to be "do not enter my business and I will stay away from yours."

This is why the Tata Group finds it easier to grow profitably outside India than compete within the country, despite the potential growth markets which foreign companies and investors are chasing in India.

The Tata Group's foreign investments are based on a strategy of seeking prestigious consumer brands and critical industrial businesses. Their successful foreign acquisitions include Jaguar, Land Rover and Tetley Tea. About 70% of the group's fiscal 2015 revenues of $109 billion came from outside India.

Since 2010, the Internet and mobile businesses have boomed in India, in part due to investments from foreign funds and business partners, including the Chinese. There is also much expectation that Prime Minister Narendra Modi will speed up India's growth by further liberalizing policies.

But Modi is finding it difficult to attract new companies to enter traditional businesses, where policies are controlled by a major Indian business group. So he is trying to strengthen rival business groups who support his growth policies.

India is very attractive, compared to China, to foreign investors and companies. They can easily pull their investments and profits out of the country. Also, foreign companies are not required to transfer their technical and intellectual knowledge to Indian partners, who could be potential rivals.

Deals with the government can be enforced since India depends on foreign investments. Contracts with Indian companies and partners have a good chance of being fulfilled if they have major assets in the U.S. or Europe and it is signed under U.S. or European law.

## Looking for Wild Elephants

Raj appointed P.K. Michael Tharakan and Chiranjib Sen as my thesis advisers at the end of the first semester. Michael, a Ph.D. student of Raj, is a leading authority on the economic history of Kerala. He was over six feet tall, well built, with a clipped goatee and a good story teller. He wore a white lungi and untucked white shirt with sandals.

I could not focus on my studies after two weeks on the campus. So I took weekend trips, including several to Kovalam, a beach about fifteen miles south of the campus.

A room at a beachfront shack, with a bed made of coir ropes, cost about Rs.20, or $2. Many of the shacks were owned by a local gangster in his 30s, secured through muscle and political power since he was able to deliver a majority of the local votes.

I watched and listened to the waves, slept on the sand, drank a couple of beers and planned the work I had to finish, when I got back to CDS.

One three-day weekend I visited the Periyar Tiger Reserve. I saw elephants, deer, bison and monkeys during a two-hour boat ride on the Periyar Lake, but no tigers. I told Michael about seeing several elephants when I got back to CDS.

He said there were no elephants in Periyar for decades since poachers had killed them. Then, in the early 1960s, the Indian Prime Minister Jawaharlal Nehru was to visit the reserve.

The forest rangers brought in wild elephants and other animals from elsewhere before Nehru's trip. Soon the growing population of elephants wandered outside the reserve, searching for food and attacking people in nearby villages.

One Saturday morning Cherian Punnathara, Mammen Chundamannil and I took a bus to go on a hike in Bonacaud. It is a 2,500-acre nature preserve of hills, valleys and a waterfall, about 40 miles from Thiruvananthapuram. It was a tea plantation, set up by the British in the late 1800s, which was shut in the 1970s after years of losses.

It rained as we walked up the hills and we stopped often to pull leeches off our feet, hands and face. We saw a variety of birds and a monkey of a rare breed. We came across fresh elephant dung on the flat grasslands, on the top of the hills, but no elephants.

I was nervous about cobras and other poisonous snakes, commonly found in Kerala, when we camped overnight in a tent.

The next day, we walked through the forest since Cherian and Mammen wanted to see wild elephants. I got nervous as we went deeper into the forest, where there was little grass or shrubs below the trees.

I said we should go back the way we came, since we did not have a compass and we might get lost. But they said we would be fine. They were seasoned hikers and campers and volunteered with nature loving groups.

I was relieved, several hours later, when we got to a road and found a bus stop. The leeches, attack by bees on a college trip and my fear of heights and getting lost have kept me away from hiking and camping trips.

**Studying the Sugar Industry under Coconut Trees**

Michael, my thesis adviser, gave me a 15-page essay "How to Write a Thesis?" which I read numerous times. In part based on this essay, I decided to structure my research around two questions: Why did sugar cooperatives succeed in Maharashtra? How do the cooperatives set the prices they pay to farmers for their sugarcane? The preliminary title for my thesis was "Sugar Cooperatives in Maharashtra: History and Sugarcane Prices."

I met Michael about every two weeks. We discussed what I had read and if it helped with the research for my thesis. While we got into lots of discussions, we never got into an argument and he never insisted I study a particular issue or angle of approach. He offered suggestions and let me explore the research on my own.

G.N. Rao, an author of studies on agriculture, was the faculty adviser to my class. He asked students if they faced any problems and how he could help. He invited us to his house for several dinners.

He taught a course on Indian agriculture during the second semester. Following India's independence, state governments passed laws to reform ownership of farmland. In most states the reforms helped farmers from the warrior and peasant caste, the Kshatriyas, to expand the farmland they owned and controlled.

The Kshatriyas are the biggest percentage of the population in most states and vote as a block. Their political and economic power mutually reinforce each other.

Many of the big farmers control larger farms than shown in the official records by hiding ownership under other names to avoid legal ceilings. They also lease land from others. Their political connections give them easier access to loans from farmers' cooperatives and other banks.

The money lenders in the village, who are from the Vaishya caste, continue to offer loans to small and medium farmers who do not have the political clout and sufficient collateral to borrow from the banks.

I wrote a term paper on the economic history of sugar cooperatives in Maharashtra. In 1982, these factories accounted for about forty percent of India's total production of 8.4 million tons.

Cooperative factories continue to produce over two thirds of the sugar in Maharashtra. In 2015, total sugar production in the state, by cooperative and private factories, was 10.5 million tons, about a third of India's output.

**Tasting Water Ducks and a Backwater Fish**

Cooperative factories in the fertile western part of the state are the biggest and most productive. My paper, and the first part of my thesis, analyzed the rise of sugarcane farming and sugar cooperatives in the western district of Ahmednagar.

The spread of canal irrigation, during the early 1900s, led to the farming of cash crops like vegetables, fruits and sugarcane. The farmers got loans to grow these crops from farmer-run cooperative banks which were expanding in the region.

The sugarcane was sold to urban traders who processed it into jaggery, an unrefined brownish raw sugar, in plants powered by bulls. The jaggery was sold in Mumbai and other cities at a huge profit over the prices paid to the farmers for their sugarcane.

In the 1920s, three sugar factories were set up in the region by traders and urban business owners. Refining sugar is more profitable than making jiggery since the price of sugar is higher, and twice as much sugar is recovered from the same volume of cane juice.

Farmers planted sugarcane in more areas with irrigation since it was a profitable and hardy crop. The collapse in global agricultural prices, during the Great Depression of the early 1930s, hurt the farmers.

Some of the farmers got together and set up cooperatively-owned mechanical jaggery production plants to capture a higher profit from processing the juice, instead of selling their sugarcane to the traders.

In 1950, farmers set up the first cooperatively owned factory, after seeing the price and volume benefits enjoyed by the private owners of sugar mills. By 1959, there were fourteen sugar cooperatives operating in Western Maharashtra; and 52 in 1981. The farmer-run factories were financed by cooperative banks.

The sugar cooperatives in Maharashtra state are mostly controlled by the Marathas. They are from the peasant and warrior caste and are about 40% of the population. They hence control the politics of the state.

Several friends from Mumbai visited me at CDS, including Charles De Souza and George Abraham. During Ajit Sanzgiri's visit, T.M. Thomas Isaac invited us to spend a day at his home in Alleppey, near the backwater canals. Isaac was a research fellow working on a Ph.D. thesis on the coir industry in Kerala.

I had heard that his mother was an exceptional cook. That morning she made appams, rice cakes made from a batter of finely hand ground rice, coconut milk and toddy, the juice drawn from the flowering buds of coconut trees.

Also poot, rice and fresh coconut steamed in a bamboo funnel. This was my favorite dish on visits to Kerala as a kid. I mixed the appams and poot with fresh coconut milk and sugar, though they also tasted good with chickpeas.

We had duck for lunch, a very tender and juicy meat since they were water ducks. For dinner, there was Karimeen, a tasty and much sought fish. They are found in the slushy depths of the backwaters in the coastal areas of Kerala. The fisherman hold their breath and dive deep to try to catch the fish.

We drank lots of fresh toddy and beer. Each meal that day was the best I have eaten in Kerala and one of the best of my life.

THE POWER OF SUGAR BARONS

## Sugar Prices and Elections

I wrote a term paper on how government agencies set the prices of agricultural products. This was to help with the second part of my thesis on the pricing of sugarcane and sugar.

I gained much information on the methodology and pricing of agricultural products by the government from research papers published by N. Krishnaji. He taught at the Indian Statistical Institute in Kolkata and was earlier on the faculty at CDS. Isaac, one of his Ph.D. students, said that Krishnaji had only one book on his table - the one he was reading.

The price of sugar is a major political barometer in India. High prices for sugar, as well as for onions in the months leading up to elections, can influence voters to reject the party in power.

The Central Government largely determines the prices for sugarcane and sugar. Each year, before the harvest, it sets a minimum floor price per ton of sugarcane to be paid to farmers, by both private and cooperative factories. Cooperatives pay an additional price to members for their sugarcane.

Both cooperative and private factories have to sell part of their sugar output – this quota was 65% in the early 1980s - to the Central Government at a set price. They can sell the rest of their produce in the open market.

The government sets the prices for sugarcane and sugar based on the cost plus method, costs for materials and production plus a rate of return, and on political considerations.

In years of shortages, the government's goal is to sell its sugar to poor and middle class consumers through a distribution system of ration shops at prices below the market price.

In years of excess production, the goal is to help farmers get the government-set minimum price for their sugarcane, which is often higher than what they would get from traders.

The government prices for sugarcane and sugar and the open market prices for sugar are publicly available. In May, after the end of the second semester at CDS, I went to Mumbai to find the missing piece of the puzzle, the sugarcane prices received by cooperative farmers.

Journalists and academics said that the farmers did not want public disclosure of the prices they got for their sugarcane since many cooperatives accumulate huge losses to pay high prices to their members. So I had little hope of finding the prices.

In Mumbai I met S.M. Gothoskar, the economist and public relations officer for the Maharashtra State Cooperative Sugar Federation. A Brahman, working for the Marathas who controlled the lobbying group, he introduced me to the economist at the Maharashtra State Co-operative Bank.

At the bank I got access to spreadsheets, with detailed annual financial data, submitted by the sugar cooperatives. I copied the data of the past ten years for the twelve sugar cooperatives operating in Ahmednagar, a district in the fertile Western region.

I considered myself lucky to get the data, but likely both the bank and the sugar lobby cared little about the impact of an academic study. They were right, as I found out later.

I got back to CDS eager to write my thesis and get it approved by my advisers by December, before the monthly fellowship payments stopped. My brother George offered to support me financially if I needed extra time with the thesis.

My thesis stated that during sugarcane and sugar shortages,

as in 1980-81, cooperatives made huge profits from selling sugar in the open market. They paid members more than double the government set minimum price for sugarcane. Cooperatives, which had major accumulated losses, did not add to reserves in such profitable years.

In years of excess sugar production, as in 1977-78, many cooperatives suffered losses. Yet they paid members 50% more than the government set minimum sugarcane price. They made such payments by reducing maintenance and capital expenditures and by borrowing from cooperative banks. One cooperative factory incurred losses in five of the seven previous years.

In 1981, twenty-one of the fifty-two cooperative factories in Maharashtra were considered "sick". They had huge accumulated losses and were not paying interest on the loans from cooperative banks. The government periodically allows the loss-making sugar cooperative factories to write off their loans to the cooperative banks, reflecting the political power of the sugar barons.

## My Best Education

I submitted my one hundred and fifty page thesis to Michael and Chiranjib in early December 1982. I was worried they may ask for more revisions and lay in bed with a cold. Ten days later, they approved the thesis, and my cold instantly vanished. I ran to a typist to get the handwritten thesis typed and bound.

I was happy I got an A-, or first class, for my M.Phil. The anonymous external referee for my thesis was likely N. Krishnaji, whose papers helped me figure out the methodology of sugarcane and sugar pricing.

The referee commented that the historical first half of my thesis "is no more than a summary of the work of other scholars."

The second half on sugarcane prices paid to cooperative

members, while original, was "more descriptive than analytical." The referee noted that it would have been helpful to compare the sugarcane prices paid by sugar cooperatives to their members to the prices paid for sugarcane by privately owned mills.

I agree with the referee's comments and would have probed the areas he mentioned, along with the business and politics of cooperatives running losses, if I had continued to study for a Ph.D.

Two research articles, based on my thesis on sugarcane pricing and economic history, were published in the *Economic & Political Weekly*. The history article has gotten some attention from academic researchers and journalists while the one on pricing has been ignored.

The economists at the sugar federation and the cooperative bank apparently knew that academic papers on sugarcane prices paid to farmers by sugar cooperatives would attract no critical attention in the media and from opposition political parties. Hence they likely gave me access to the financial data.

The M.Phil. at CDS was my best education. I learned much about the business economics of agricultural and commodity products, the impact of politics on business and the relevance of economic and business history. The method of grading students, through papers and a thesis, was a superior way to learn, especially when compared to sitting for one-shot final exams.

I remember much of my work at CDS due to the reading, reflecting, analyzing, condensing and writing for my papers and thesis. I also remember the methods: identify and analyze key issues and base analysis and conclusions on data and facts.

I made friends, recharged myself and gained confidence. Chandan, Gulati, Michael, Rajaram, Rao and Vaidhyanathan were good role models for an academic career.

But I did not want to pursue a Ph.D. at CDS. I returned to Mumbai eager to find a job in journalism.

Chapter 11

# HINDU-MUSLIM VIOLENCE FOR

# POLITICAL GAINS

I was at least five years older than most journalists starting their careers in India. So I searched for a job in Mumbai that would enable me to quickly move up the editorial hierarchy.

Meanwhile, I wrote several freelance articles. I did not mail them, but handed them to Feroz Chandra, Darryl D'Monte, Adil Jussawalla, Vinod Mehta, M.K.B. Nair, Rahul Singh, Olga Tellis, Dilip Thakore and Dina Vakil. These editors at newspaper and magazines, who at first did not know me, published most of the articles I submitted.

While waiting for a job in journalism, I worked for four months as a consultant to an agency of the Ministry of Industry in New Delhi. I collected data for setting prices for sugarcane and sugar in Maharashtra and Gujarat. I had little interest in the work since the major decisions appeared to have already been made by the political ministers.

I likely disappointed the director of the agency and also hurt the reputation of Rajaram Dasgupta. I was recommended for the job by Rajaram, my quiet neighbor at CDS.

## Choosing a Job in Journalism

My M.Phil. and over forty articles in major Indian publications on politics, economics, interviews, film and book reviews, including Gabriel Garcia Marquez's *Chronicles of a Death Foretold*, got me job offers from *The Indian Express, The Economic Times* and *The Economic & Political Weekly (EPW)*.

The *EPW* paid the least and offered the least exposure since it had a small circulation of 10,000 and a readership of about 50,000, through academic libraries. But I would learn a great deal very quickly, due to a small editorial staff. Also, given its good reputation, I could later find a senior job at a large and better paying publication.

The editor Krishna Raj hired me as an assistant editor after checking on my work with Gulati, who wrote a column on international finance for the weekly. So my term paper for Gulati at CDS was helpful, despite the B grade.

Under Raj, Nigel and Tirril Harris wrote in their obituary of him in 2004 for *The Guardian* "The *EPW* remained true to its serious purpose, its research base and policy concern, its internationalism and its openness. As a weekly, it could publish annually an immense amount of material, and such was its status that the young queued up for the honor of writing for it, alongside the great names of Indian scholarship."

Every day around 11:00 a.m., after reading the newspapers, Raj, Gautam Navlakha and I would meet and discuss news items to comment upon or get coverage from a freelance writer. Raj sought unique perspectives on major current topics as well as coverage of issues that could become big but got brief mention in newspapers.

Raj had strong opinions but was open to other viewpoints,

provided they were based on facts and logic. He probed staff and visitors by asking question after question. I try to follow this technique though without having Raj's skills.

I wrote two or three comments each week, of about 300 words, on economic, business and political topics, including on textiles, cement, steel, cotton, jute, coconut oil and electric power.

I analyzed both the economics and the political issues related to these businesses since they are impacted by government policy and since government-run corporations play major roles in many industries in India. I quickly realized that the basics of business economics and politics I learned during my M. Phil., apply universally.

For instance, while shipping volume at Indian ports grew from 63 million tons in fiscal year 1978-79 to 77 million tons two years later, the volume carried by Indian shipping companies fell by a tenth. This was due to rising Indian exports of iron ore to Japan, which were shipped in Japanese vessels.

## Saved from Drowning

Raj was a good employer, offering housing loans to employees, celebrating birthdays and being flexible about working hours. He also shared complimentary invitations to conferences, meetings and cultural events with his employees.

He gave me tickets to the Film Festival in Mumbai. The tickets could be scalped for large sums since there was huge demand for a couple of foreign films with sex scenes, which would have been cut by India's film censor board if shown commercially.

Costa-Gavras, whose films won three Oscar nominations and include political thrillers "Missing" and "Z," was one of the big names at the festival. One morning I walked into a festival public relations room, at the President Hotel on Cuffe Parade, and told

Gavras I had come to interview him for a local paper. He agreed to chat though I had no prior appointment. I had not spoken to any editor about the story.

The film maker is "an easily accessible and friendly person," I wrote in the interview published in *The Indian Express*. His films "Missing" and "State of Siege" are set in Latin America, and so I was surprised he had not visited the continent.

Gavras, discussed being labelled a left-wing filmmaker. He said "Marxism too has become a religion like…Christianity. There is a big danger if people have a religious attitude towards politics…Just as a religious man does not question god, (politicians) want citizens to blindly obey the politician."

In April 1984, Navroz Seervai and I went to New Delhi to attend the wedding of Manoj Mehra, a fellow student from Elphinstone College.

We stayed with Harish Bhonsle. He had studied English, was elected head of the college's day students council, got an MBA from the Bajaj Institute at Mumbai University and worked for Hong Kong Bank in New Delhi.

At the wedding, we saw Manoj ride up in a horse to meet his future bride Preeti and watched the Hindu ceremony, performed around a fire.

Early next morning, Harish drove us and a couple of his friends to the swimming pool at the Qutab Hotel. I cannot swim and so I splashed my way towards the deep end along the right side. I expected to be easily able to reach and hold the top edge of the pool in case I had problems.

Suddenly, as if in a dream, I found myself sinking and air bubbles rising from my nose. Even if it is a dream I should not drown, I told myself. I tried to grab the pool's sidewall but could not reach it.

I shut my mouth to avoid inhaling water. My last thoughts were unhappiness about ruining the wedding and creating problems for my mother and siblings.

The next thing I recall is hearing one of Harish's friend say, "I know a doctor at the AIIMS Hospital. Let's take him there."

Later, I spoke to Harish and Navroz to find out about the chain of events leading to my rescue.

Harish was the last to change and, walking towards the pool, he saw Navroz and his friends chatting at the shallow end. He did not see me and thought it was odd, and so shouted "Where is Iggy?" Someone in the group said, "He must have gone to the restroom." This made Harish more suspicious since he had just come from the changing room and hadn't seen me there.

Harish walked all around the pool looking for me. Then, as Harish describes, "as I got to the deepest end, to my shock and horror, I saw a body lying flat and motionless facing upwards at the bottom of the pool. Not being the strongest of swimmers, I waved and shouted frantically for help."

There was no lifeguard on duty and no one in our group was strong enough to rescue me.

"A man came running, from a lounge chair on the lawn, dived in, lifted and placed you on the pool's edge. He then started pumping your chest. After roughly twenty minutes, you coughed up some blood and that was probably the first sign you may have been saved," says Harish.

An ambulance took me to a hospital. I stayed in a hospital for a day and missed the wedding reception.

In the chaos and confusion, none of us got the name and contact information of the man who saved my life. Harish says he was Eastern European.

## Finding the Limits of Journalism

In May 1984, over 250 people were killed in clashes between Hindus and Muslims in and around Mumbai, many of them poor Muslims on their way to work. I wrote a two-page story, "Unlearnt Lesson of 1970," for the weekly. I argued that such clashes are triggered for political and economic goals.

In 1966, Bal Thackeray, a newspaper cartoonist, started the Shiv Sena political party in Mumbai. He demanded that 80% of the jobs in Maharashtra be reserved for Maharashtrians.

Sena groups burnt restaurants and businesses run by South Indians, and buses, trains and other government property. As an eleven-year-old, walking home from school, I saw smoke rising near the Kalina bus stop. A booth had been burnt by a gang led by a construction contractor. It was used by a government dairy to sell pasteurized milk in refrigerated bottles.

The Sena was feared in Mumbai and grew popular among Maharashtrians. But, by the early 1980s, it was a minor political force due to reports of corruption, a gangster image, its opposing a strike by state government employees in 1974 and its support for Prime Minister Indira Gandhi's dictatorial rule from 1975 to 1977.

In 1984, the Sena leaders sought to revive and broaden the party's appeal by claiming to protect Hindus from attacks by Muslims. The clashes started after a rumor that some Muslims had insulted the Sena leader Thackeray by putting a garland of shoes around his photograph.

One afternoon, near the end of the two weeks of clashes, filmmaker Saeed Mirza and I went to the Kherwadi and Nagpada areas in Central Mumbai where many were killed. We were in the Muslim part when we heard police sirens.

Very quickly large crowds of men and boys gathered on opposite sides of a narrow road, while the women, children and the elderly watched from windows and balconies. We joined the crowd hearing that Prime Minister Indira Gandhi was visiting the area.

Several police cars arrived with their sirens blaring. Indira Gandhi got out of a white Ambassador car, with tinted windows, about ten feet from where we stood.

She faced and greeted the Muslim crowd with folded hands, accepted garlands and flowers and got back in the car and left. The Muslims clapped and cheered loudly.

Fifteen feet away, on the other side of the road, the large crowd of Hindus began chanting slogans against Indira Gandhi, upset she had snubbed them. There were hundreds of policemen on the road, many carrying rifles.

Yet the tension between the two groups was so high that anyone moving a few feet across the road would have been instantly attacked, setting off another round of killings.

A few minutes later, a second batch of police cars arrived. Rajiv Gandhi, the Prime Minister's son, got out of a car on the Hindu side. He greeted the crowd, accepted garlands and flowers and left. The Hindus clapped and cheered, and the crowds vanished in minutes.

In 1970, Hindu-Muslim clashes in Bhiwandi, near Mumbai, led to 78 deaths. An official inquiry was conducted by D.P. Madon, a judge of the Bombay High Court. His report stated that the Hindu parties, Shiv Sena and Bharatiya Jana Sangh, and a Muslim group were responsible for the killings. But no one was prosecuted. The Sangh is now the Bharatiya Janata Party headed by Prime Minister Narendra Modi.

My story had no policy impact, nor did it lead to a wider debate. I hence admire the courage of Sunil Gavaskar, a Hindu and Maharashtrian and one of India's greatest cricketers. He reportedly walked out of his residential building and rescued a Muslim being attacked by a Hindu mob during the 1992 clashes in Mumbai. Over 900 were killed in those clashes, two thirds of them Muslim.

## The Politics of Hindu-Muslim Clashes

Hindu-Muslim clashes continue to occur regularly. Today the trigger can be opinions and images posted online, which are seen as major religious insults. In the pre-Internet days, clashes often started after the head of a cow was found in a temple or when a pig was thrown into a mosque.

Such clashes played a part in the May 2014 election of Prime Minister Narendra Modi's Bharatiya Janata Party (BJP.) Sanjeev Balyan's "presence in the cabinet is a reminder that stoking such (Hindu-Muslim) divisions remains a way to win votes," and political power, wrote Ellen Barry and Suhasini Raj, in a 2014 *New York Times* article, "Amid Modi's Centrist Shift, an Aide with a Turbulent Past Rises."

Balyan is a veterinarian and junior minister for agriculture in Modi's government. He won election to parliament for precisely one thing: rallying the Jats, a Hindu peasant and warrior caste, to attack Muslims. The clashes, in his district in Uttar Pradesh, started over moving a bicycle and the killing of two Hindu men and a Muslim man.

A police report about the inflaming of a Hindu crowd by Balyan and other leaders from his party summarized their words: "Wherever we will find…the Muslim community, by killing them, we will get our revenge." About sixty people were killed, mostly Muslims, and tens of thousands of Muslims fled their homes.

*The New York Times* story did not report if the business, farms, homes and other property of the Muslims were taken over by the Hindus.

This economic aspect of the clashes is shown in *Garam Hawa* (Scorching Winds), a film by M.S. Sathyu. It is a story about Hindu rivals destroying the leather business and taking over the large family house of a Muslim, who decided to stay on in India, after the partition with Pakistan in 1947.

Muslim religious and political leaders also set off clashes to expand their influence among Muslims. There are also Muslim criminal gangs who seek to expand their power during such clashes. But Muslims fare badly since the police force is made up of Hindus who openly support the Hindu mobs, as Judge Madon noted in his report.

## The Caste Divide Among Hindus

The Hindu parties like the BJP are mostly supported by the upper castes. The lower castes face violent attacks from the upper castes and so typically do not support Hindu parties.

In 2014, according to official figures, 744 Dalits were killed and over 2,200 Dalit women were raped by upper caste Hindu men. The real numbers were likely higher since many do not make police complaints for fear of further attacks.

The Dalits are the lower castes of Hindus, also known as the scheduled castes. About fifteen percent of government and semi-government jobs and seats at medical and other professional colleges are reserved for them. The Dalits hence support political parties which are not tied to the upper castes and which will protect their college and job quotas

The upper caste Hindus are often divided over quotas for colleges and jobs. In the summer of 2015, for instance, the Patels in Gujarat held huge protests in which ten people were killed. They opposed reserved quotas for the Dalits and backward castes in professional colleges and government jobs.

The backward castes are mainly sub-castes of the peasant and warrior upper caste. The Patels are also upper caste - land and business owners who make up about 10% of Gujarat's population.

Their votes and funding were major factors in electing Narendra Modi as chief minister of Gujarat, before he was elected Prime Minister of India.

Similarly in Haryana, in February 2016, Jats blocked roads and railways and cut off water supply to Delhi. They were seeking reserved quotas in professional colleges and jobs. The Jats are a peasant and warrior caste who make up about a quarter of the state's population.

The army was brought in to protect the water supply and control the violent crowds. The violence stopped after the BJP government in the state agreed to grant the quotas sought by the Jat leaders. It also gave $15,000 to the families of nineteen people who died during the protests.

The BJP government gave in to the demands since the party needs the votes of the Jats to get elected. But this makes the other sub-castes fear that their job and college quotas will be reduced.

Such conflicts among the upper castes split Hindu votes. So Hindu parties will continue to provoke Hindu-Muslim clashes to attract support as protectors of all Hindus.

Hindu groups have also attacked Christians for converting Hindus to Christianity.

Should Christians stop doing humanitarian work "for being so admired and loved that a stray beneficiary converts of his or her own accord?" wrote Julio Ribeiro in *The Indian Express*, following attacks on Christian churches and schools in Delhi in 2015. A Christian and former head of police in Mumbai, he headed the police force in Punjab in 1986, which protected Hindus from attacks by Sikh separatists.

"I am not an Indian anymore, at least in the eyes of the proponents of the Hindu Rashtra (nation). Is it coincidence or a well-thought-out plan that the ... targeting of a small and peaceful community should begin only after the BJP government of Narendra Modi came to power," Ribeiro added.

### Chatting with *Newsweek's* Cultural Editor

*EPW*'s office was in a modest building near a train terminal, now named after the Maharashtrian King Shivaji. It was a long clean room, with tall metal book racks forming cubicles. The tables were piled high with books, newspapers, reports of government agencies, World Bank and International Monetary Fund reports and articles submitted for consideration of publication.

The weekly attracted several visitors each day, academics and journalists from India and abroad. Some came to research old *EPW* issues and others to chat with Raj.

He was generous with his time, offering tea and suggesting they review a book or write a piece. A select few, whom Raj called "friends of the weekly," were invited to the Mumbai Press club for beer and snacks in the evening.

Charles Michener, a former cultural editor of *Newsweek*, visited the office one morning. He had heard from Indian journalists that the weekly was a good source to do research for his upcoming interview with Indira Gandhi.

She was re-elected Prime Minister in 1980 after causing a split in the previous government. Her Congress Party supported a leader of a faction in the ruling Janata party to become Prime Minister. She withdrew support a month later, and fresh elections were held. Her Congress Party won a majority of seats in parliament due to the splintering of opposition votes.

Raj invited Gautam and me to join in the chat with Charles. I asked Charles about President Reagan's popularity in the U.S., the appeal of Michael Jackson and how American policy makers viewed India and its non-aligned strategy of not joining either

Soviet Union or U.S. -led alliances.

Charles said I should meet him while he was in Mumbai. I called and met him after overcoming doubts that he invited me just to be polite.

He suggested I apply to the journalism school at Columbia in New York. He said he had studied there and would recommend me to Osborn Elliott, the dean of the school. Dean Elliott was his editor at *Newsweek*.

This chance meeting with Charles pushed me to apply to the school, something I was contemplating. I got help in writing the application essays from Gopal Kamat, who had returned after an MBA from Cornell.

In April 1985, I got a letter from the school saying I had been admitted. The letter also said that I "must be able to type a minimum of thirty five words a minute." The school gave me a grant of $4,500 and a loan of $3000, at 5% annual interest.

The funds from the school covered only a third of the $22,000 in tuition, boarding and other costs. I typed and mailed letters to hundreds of endowments and foundations in India and the U.S., seeking grants and loans to fund the gap.

Some foundations, which were run by families of Elphinstone students I knew, ignored my request. I applied to the Tata Endowment after an introduction to its director from Navroz Seervai, an Elphinstone College alumnus.

The Tata family funds the endowment, several hospitals, an institute for fundamental science and mathematics research and also clean water, literacy, healthcare and other social, educational and cultural programs.

The funds for these operations come from eleven philanthropic foundations which own 66% of Tata Sons, the parent company of the Tata Group. The Tata family, who like Navroz are Parsis, own three percent of the group. The family and the group's business managers have the best reputation for integrity and ethical conduct among Indian businesses.

I got a $2,000 loan, at 5% interest, and a $500 grant from Tata, a $800 loan at 2% interest from the R.D. Sethna Trust, also Parsi run, and a grant for an air ticket to New York.

But even with these my school costs were only half funded. I was nervous that my U.S. student visa application would be rejected due to the funding gap and also not owning real estate and other major assets in India.

Ashok Mahadevan, editor of the *Readers' Digest India* and a Columbia journalism school alumnus, introduced me to other alumni in the U.S. to help find additional funds.

One prospect was a grant of a semester's fees from the New York based India Abroad Foundation. But the grant was given only after an Indian student reached New York and was enrolled at the school. This was of no help in getting a U.S. visa.

In the papers submitted for the visa, I included a character reference letter from Homai Shroff, a former head of Elphinstone College. She was a popular English teacher, respected by both students and staff for being a fair administrator.

I was not in any of her classes but she knew me from my student politics, including the meeting on the campus which led to Durga Bhagwat's arrest during the State of Emergency.

I got the visa and flew to New York. An admission official at the Columbia Journalism School said she was surprised that I showed up. She assumed I would not be able to raise the funds and get a visa to study in the U.S.

## Chapter 12

## A TINY WIDGET IN A CAPITALIST TOOL

I took up a full-time job at *India Abroad,* after graduating from the journalism school. I was paid $7.50 an hour. The newspaper's foundation repaid a $3,000 student loan I got from Columbia.

### "Wheatish Complexion" in Matrimonial ads

The weekly newspaper's office was a large open space with high ceilings, on the full floor of a building with a freight elevator on 24th street, between Broadway and Sixth Avenue.

The other tenants in the building, as well is in the buildings nearby, were importers and wholesalers of apparel, fabrics, cheap jewelry and handbags.

At night there were few people on the streets, and I walked fast to the number 1 subway station at Seventh Avenue, constantly looking behind. A couple of candy stores run by Indians, a Korean run grocery, an Irish bar and a Greek diner were the only stores open after 6:00 p.m. on 23rd Street.

Today, considered part of Chelsea, the area has offices of major web, advertising and technology businesses, new high rise residential buildings, food retailers like Eataly and Trader Joe's and expensive bars and restaurants. Commercial and residential real estate prices in Chelsea has had the highest appreciation in New York City since I arrived in 1985.

*India Abroad* had a circulation of about 40,000 in the U.S. and Canada, mostly recurring annual subscriptions of about $40 each. The 32-page tabloid carried more advertising than editorial pages. The business was run with a small, low paid staff of Indians and was apparently very profitable.

Classified advertising brought in the most revenue, with matrimonial advertisements being the biggest section, eight or more pages roughly equally divided between search for brides and grooms. The ads were placed by parents and relatives in keeping with the Indian tradition of arranged marriages.

The ads listed the age, education and jobs of the men and women in the U.S. and Canada and some from India. Suitors with good education, jobs and character, from respectable families and the same religion and caste, were asked to mail photos and biographies to a post box at *India Abroad*.

Many of the ads seeking husbands said the women had a "wheatish complexion," pointing to the lighter skin favored by Indians. Most of the ads seeking brides said the men were either engineers, doctors or executives.

The rise of online media and websites has wiped out classified ads from the print edition of *India Abroad*. Its online edition lists matrimonial ads but most such ads have moved to new websites like *Shaadi* (wedding).

### Business Plan for an Indian Magazine

I was keen to start my own publication and wrote a plan and an outline of the content for the first three issues for *IndiaInc*, a monthly newsletter aimed at Indian professionals and business owners in the U.S. They were mainly engineers and doctors or Patels from Gujarat, who owned candy stores and motels, giving rise to the term motel Patels.

Indian executives were rising into the ranks of upper tier management at large American companies. Several engineers were leaving major firms to start information technology companies.

The Indian population in the U.S. was roughly a million in the mid-1980s. It was expanding in part due to about 25,000 Indians arriving each year to study at American universities.

The newsletter was to be upgraded to a color magazine, as circulation and revenues grew. It would also grow to reach Indians in Canada, Europe and the Middle East.

The long term goals were to expand into book publishing, distribution of magazines and books from India, syndicating articles to the press in India, conducting market studies and providing consulting help for U.S. firms seeking business in India.

I showed the business plan to several Indian professionals. But I was unable to raise $60,000, the estimated cost for a part-time editor and reporter for the first year. I did not show the plan to Gopal Raju, who owned *India Abroad*, or Indian businessmen, fearing they would copy the plan.


The trends of Indians climbing corporate ladders and starting businesses have sharply accelerated. The list of former and current Indian chief executives include Sundar Pichai at Google, Satya Nadella at Microsoft, Shantanu Narayen at software vendor Adobe, Indra Nooyi at Pepsico, Surya Mohapatra at medical testing firm Quest Diagnostics and Rakesh Sachdev of chemicals and bio-chemicals supplier Sigma-Aldrich.

Successful major companies founded by Indians in the U.S. include Sun Microsystems, Hotmail, Cascade Communications and TIBCO Software. (My essay discussing this success, "Indian Entrepreneurs in the U.S.," is in Appendix C.)

Meanwhile, at *India Abroad* I argued with an editor when he shouted at me for including a brief four-line story. Perhaps he was annoyed I was not seeking career advice from him.

The owner Raju cut my hours by half, and my income fell to $150 a week. I paid $200 in monthly rent for a bedroom in an apartment in Washington Heights, shared with three other Columbia graduates, and so I was OK. But I did not have health insurance coverage.

I met Pavan Sahgal, editor of *The Wall Street Computer Review*, seeking freelance stories. He was a Bagehot fellow and alumnus of the journalism school at Columbia and a former editor of *India Abroad*. I was introduced to him by Ashok Mahadevan.

I wrote several stories for the monthly, a color magazine covering the use of technology by Wall Street firms. I interviewed executives of vendors and users and wrote on the power and use of parallel computers, the potential demand for self-learning expert software systems and the expanding role of chief information officers at major Wall Street firms.

I understood nothing of the technical issues, but the fees were good: $600 for 1,200 words and $1,200 for 2,500 words.

### Business Insights from Flea Markets

On weekends I helped a couple of vendors who were selling at flea markets. We bought sweaters, scarves, gloves, earrings, bracelets and brass candlesticks and vases, made in China, South Korea and India, from wholesalers near Macy's.

Around 6:30 a.m. on Saturdays we paid $20 and rented a

spot for a table in the yard of the Robert Louis Stevenson School on 67th Street between First and York Avenues. On Sundays, we set up a table in the yard of Middle School 44 on Columbus Avenue between 76th and 77th Street.

There were indoor spots at both schools, useful during severely cold days in December. But they were reserved for vendors who sold at the market for several years. Any indoor spots available, when a regular vendor did not show up, were given by the managers of the markets to new vendors who gave them $20 or more in tips.

Customers bought jewelry, art and photographs, lace imported from Europe and other expensive items from the indoor vendors at Stevenson. One vendor was a Gujarati who sold over $150,000 in Indian gold and silver jewelry a year.

I saw the French actress Catherine Deneuve shopping at the Stevenson market. Vendors there also recalled that Andy Warhol spent hours going through their inventory.

We displayed our goods on a roughly 6 feet by 3 feet folding table in the yard, amid vendors of cakes, sausages, vegetables, apples and cheap jewelry and apparel. We priced the goods from $3 to $20, based on the retail prices in stores, competing vendors and discounts for multiple purchases. Our markup over wholesale prices ranged from 50% to 200%.

Displaying our goods attractively and informing customers of the big discount in our prices, compared to retail stores, was helpful in making sales. Earrings and bracelets, in the $3 to $5 range, sold quickly.

There was little demand for the extra extra large and small sized sweaters, which made up a fifth of the wholesale packs. They were also bulky to transport in a car and to store. So we kept cutting their prices till they sold and used the money to buy quick selling jewelry and brass items.

Some customers came to socialize, including one at

Stevenson who wanted to chat about India since her daughter was living there. We had good sales on sunny days and weak sales on cold days. The vendors selling coffee, bagels and muffins did good business on all days since the other vendors bought more coffee and food on cold days.

I was reminded of the good business of the coffee vendors years later, while working as an investment analyst. I read that vendors of clothing, food and liquor did good business during the Gold Rush in California in the 1840's and 1850's. The jeans maker Levi Strauss & Co. and the chocolatier Ghirardelli are still around while the gold mining companies disappeared.

The best sales were from the week before Thanksgiving to Christmas eve. During the week before Christmas we rented a table space at an arts and crafts fair on the sidewalk alongside Bryant Park on 42nd Street. The fair was meant for artisans to sell their hand-crafted goods but most vendors were selling manufactured goods, including from China and India.

Our inventory was sold out by the evening each day, and by 1:00 p.m. on Christmas Eve, given the crowds on the street. Today, dozens of temporary stores sell art, scarves, chocolates and apple cider in Bryant Park during the weeks before Christmas.

After Christmas, we sold scarves and gloves, but the profits were small since there were several competitors and there was not much demand. The next big sales for jewelry and gift items was in early February, before Valentine's Day.

I learned a great deal about operating a business during the six months I spent at the flea markets: purchasing, pricing, sales, managing inventory and cash, quality, convenience and service.

Today, the two flea markets have only a few vendors selling fruits, vegetables, bread, sausages and cheap apparel. Their business has been hit by online markets like eBay and Etsy, where jewelry, antiques, surplus apparel and hand-crafted goods are sold.

Customers can easily find online a wide choice of vendors, better pricing information and vendor ratings. Vendors can reach buyers anywhere, track a competitor's prices and source from around the world.

### Fact Checking About American Business

I continued to write freelance stories for *The Wall Street Computer Review* during weekdays, working from libraries at Columbia University. Every two months, I mailed copies of my recent articles to Jean Briggs at *Forbes,* while saying I remained interested in a job at the magazine. I also sent the articles to editors at other publications, seeking a job.

In April 1987, while I was planning a trip to Europe on my way back to Mumbai, Jean Briggs asked if I was interested in interviewing for a temporary job for six months. I was hired by *Forbes,* after a couple of interviews. I started by fact checking stories for the bi-weekly's Science & Technology section.

Gary Samuels, the section's editor, needed two or three stories for each issue. But few writers or even fact checkers were interested in writing for the section. So he assigned me articles.

The six-month position was a tryout. When it was over, Jean hired me as a reporter at a salary of $20,000 a year. I hence had to pay an immigration lawyer twice for the work visas I got through *Forbes.*

In September 1988, I joined a team for a new Computer & Communications section at the magazine. Rival *Businessweek* had a similar section which carried advertising from major information technology and telecom companies.

The 1980s and the early 1990s were the golden age for print business publishers in the U.S., with *Fortune, Businessweek* and

*Forbes*, niche ones like *Venture, Inc.* and *Worth*, regional titles like *Crain's* and numerous trade publications in addition to *The Wall Street Journal*. They enjoyed financial success since their issues were packed with paying advertisers.

Each issue of *Forbes* was over two hundred pages, with over half the pages carrying color ads. The magazine's annual special issues, like the List of 400 wealthiest people, Mutual Funds and Top 400 companies, had several hundred pages of ads.

*Forbes*, marketed as The Capitalist Tool, was the *People* magazine of the business world. It's one and two page opinionated stories, with lots of color photographs, celebrated the business and financial success of entrepreneurs, chief executives and investors.

Its columnists gave advice on how to profit and avoid losses, when investing in stocks, bonds, real estate and collectibles.

The magazine carried a few critical pieces, especially on financial scam artists, though rarely on car companies and other major advertisers.

The 2013 Martin Scorsese film "The Wolf of Wall Street" refers to a 1991 *Forbes* story about the penny stock operator played by Leonardo DiCaprio. The story was written by a reporter Roula Khalaf, now the Foreign Editor of *The Financial Times*.

The magazine, run as an enterprising family business, had energetic, ambitious journalists, some with difficult personalities. It sponsored foreigners for work visas and hired reporters with no journalism experience. They included MBAs as well as Ph.D.s, like reporter Paul Klebnikov who got a doctorate from the London School of Economics. He was shot dead in Moscow in 2004, while editor of *Forbes Russia,* an unsolved murder.

*Forbes* paid the least among major business publications, and several writers and editors were fired each year. They were under pressure to produce stories for each issue. One assistant managing editor had a whiteboard in his office listing writers working under him and their stories published year to date.

Writers did not publish books while at the magazine, unlike at *Fortune* and *Businessweek*, for fear of losing their jobs.

The reporters at *Forbes*, lowest in the editorial hierarchy, viewed their job as training to find better, stable jobs at other business magazines and major newspapers. The reporters were in turn, reminded by a senior editor that the savings on the insurance coverage against lawsuits, gotten with a system of fact checking, more than covered the cost of hiring fact checkers. Many of the reporters at *Forbes* went on to successful journalism and careers in other fields.

I found fact checking to be an easy job when the writers were methodical and had good sources, like the late Jim Cook and Jerry Flint. But I got into major arguments while checking stories of writers who did sloppy work and of reporters with limited knowledge of the material, but eager to move up the ladder.

I misspelled the name of the investment bank IBJ Schroder by adding an extra "e," while fact checking a quarter-page story in Streetwalker, the section on investment tips. The senior editor, who wrote the story, complained to Jean about my error.

I fact-checked a story, written by Laura Jereski, for which *Forbes* was sued. The court dismissed the lawsuit stating that the article was constitutionally protected "because it consists of opinion free of material errors." The ruling noted that as a second reporter, with an economics background fact checking the article, I "made inquiries and reviewed sources."

Laura, a fellow reporter, went on to work for *The Wall Street Journal* and *Businessweek*. She won the Gerald Loeb Award, the leading prize for business journalists, and was a finalist for a Pulitzer Prize.

She left journalism to work as an analyst at fund manager Tweedy Browne, a noted value investor. She is now an adjunct professor at Fordham Law School.

I got bylines for over twenty stories, meaning I reported

them but they were rewritten by editors with *Forbes* strong one-sided opinions.

I wrote about the founder of drug dispensing company Alza Corp getting another chance to succeed; Northern Telecom using profits from its protected home market in Canada to expand globally; the success of MetPath, a pioneer in mail order medical testing, due to its focus on service, technology and scale; and Novell's Ray Noorda figuring out early that software and systems, to hook up personal computers into networks, would become more profitable than selling networking hardware.

But some of my stories were rejected by the editors. They said the articles were dull and dry like an analyst's research report.

## Chapter 13

## AN INVESTMENT ANALYST

## ON WALL STREET

I was eager to find an intellectually challenging and stimulating job. I had no interest in spending decades trying to climb up the editorial ladder at a magazine or a daily newspaper.

I asked senior writers at *Forbes*, who covered Wall Street and investing, how I could learn about finance. They said I should get an MBA.

A reporter at *Forbes* got a job on Wall Street, after a part-time MBA from the Stern School at New York University. I assumed that an MBA from a top business school would provide the keys to unlock the secrets of finance and Wall Street.

While reporting stories for *Forbes*, I spoke to analysts at major Wall Street firms. They wrote reports on public companies which were sold to institutional investors. I realized, during such conversations, that analyzing the business of companies was similar to my research on the sugar industry for my M.Phil. thesis.

I met five Wall Street analysts to find out how I could get a job as a junior analyst. Richard Schwarz invited me for a sandwich lunch at his desk near the large trading floor at Shearson Lehman Hutton. He was much older than most sell side analysts, who were in their late twenties and early thirties.

He said that firms hire MBAs with industry experience as analysts. I had neither qualification, and so he asked if I knew any senior sales executives at Wall Street firms, who could recommend me for a job. I said I did not.

I was annoyed at Schwarz for politely saying he could not help me since I assumed there must be demand for good research. Later, while working at SoGen funds, I found he was right since a good sales force is far more important than good analysts for Wall Street firms.

**Stumbling upon Warren Buffett and Value Investing**

*Forbes* gave its editorial staff free copies of *The Wall Street Journal, Businessweek* and *Fortune*. I also read *The Financial Times, The New York Times* and *The Economist* and borrowed books on business and finance from the library.

In 1988, I stumbled upon an article "The Inside Story of Warren Buffett" by Carol Loomis in *Fortune* in 1988. The only thing I knew about Buffett was that he was on the *Forbes* 400 List, due to his holdings of Berkshire Hathaway stock.

Loomis described Buffett's success as an owner of businesses and as an investor in public securities, based on value investing: analyzing the long term economics of a business and buying $1 of assets for fifty cents.

I wrote to Berkshire, got its annual reports and read Buffett's analysis of businesses and investments in his letters to shareholders.

"Buffett's approach to investment involves using seventh grade math and common sense," I wrote while reviewing Alice Schroeder's insightful biography, *The Snowball: Warren Buffett and the Business of Life* for *Knowledge@Wharton* in 2009.

My research on the business economics of the sugar industry, analytical comments on business for the *Economic & Political Weekly* and working at flea markets gave me insights into analyzing investments.

I understood supply, demand, price, volume, competition, peaks and troughs in a cyclical business as well as the higher profit margins enjoyed by a business with a strong competitive position.

I immediately got hooked on value investing. It was an intellectual puzzle, based on analyzing data and facts. Being right or wrong in this work is clearly evident from an investment gaining or losing money.

I also liked seeking bargains, having imbibed it as a kid by observing my grandmother at bazaars in Mumbai. And a job in investing offered me a path to setting up my business in the future.

But I did not want to spend two more years in school for an MBA, taking on over $100,000 in school loans. I would be 35 when I finished my MBA, nine years older than entry level analysts. Also, since I did not know advanced math, I feared I would get low scores on the GMAT exam and not get into a top business school.

I had read about Buffett's major gains in the publishing business, through his purchase of *The Buffalo News* and stock of *The Washington Post.* So, instead of pursing an MBA and finding a job in investment research, I decided to combine my interest in investing and my journalism background and find a job in the publishing business.

## Business Plan for a Computer Magazine

I had lunch with Osborn Elliott, dean of the Columbia journalism school and former editor of *Newsweek*. I told Dean Oz, as he was called, that I was looking for a job in publishing. He asked if I was switching from journalism to make more money.

He introduced me to Robert Riordan, chairman of Family Media and a former publisher of *Newsweek*. Riordan had made a reported $84 million in profit from selling the *Ladies Home Journal* to the Meredith Corporation in 1985. He owned *Discover, Health, Model* and other magazines and had recently bought a group of trade publications, including *Computer Decisions*.

At *Forbes* I wore pleated cotton trousers, cotton shirts, tweed jackets and striped ties, bought from "antique" (used) clothing stores in the West Village. I wore loafers from LL Bean while some of the *Forbes* male staff wore wing tip shoes and yellow ties, the power attire of the 1980's.

I bought a blended light wool blue suit for $280, from a discount men's clothing store in Union Square, for my meeting with Riordan.

He asked me to write a business proposal for refreshing *Computer Decisions*, a trade magazine. It carried slightly modified press releases from hardware and software vendors. It was mailed free to executives in the computer industry and at IT companies and got its revenues from advertising and conferences.

I submitted a 12-page proposal to Riordan in early 1989. It said that 38 of 40 publications covering the computer business were trade publications. They were aimed at engineers at vendor firms and the IT managers of companies.

The revised *Computer Decisions* would be written in a colorful style with photographs of people, not machines. It would analyze short and long term trends in user needs and evaluate computers, telephones, faxes and copiers from the viewpoint of a user with little or no knowledge of the underlying technology.

My proposal said the magazine would interest senior business and finance managers at companies, who make the major buying decisions but don't have the time or expertise to go through dozens of specialized publications. It would also be read by executives and engineers at computer and IT services companies, investors in technology companies and Wall Street analysts.

*Businessweek* and *Fortune* started computer and IT sections to pursue this opportunity and *Forbes* was following them. The February 27, 1989 issue of *Businessweek* had 77 pages of advertising, roughly half of its total pages. It was a special issue on mutual funds and so had several advertisements from fund companies. Yet 40% of the ad pages were from vendors of computers, copiers, faxes and telephone services.

Riordan passed my plan to his son, who ran the trade publications. The son asked me to meet the publisher, who was brief and showed little interest. The publisher, who was in his 30s like me, must have seen me as a rival for his job. I wrote and called several times but never heard back from him or the Riordans. Later, in 1991, the Family Media business was forced to shut down due to heavy debts and a drop in advertising, during the recession.

**Lucky with my First Stock Purchases**

I went back to seeking a stock analyst's job, this time in fund management. I read Benjamin Graham's *The Intelligent Investor*, Philip Fisher's *Common Stocks and Uncommon Profits* and books by the fund manager Peter Lynch and journalist John Train.

I attended a class at the Columbia Business School taught by Bruce Greenwald. He invited major value fund managers like Mario Gabelli and Michael Price to talk about their methods and career paths.

I met Roger Murray, who taught at the school, and was one of the writers who updated *Security Analysis*, the bible of value investing written by Benjamin Graham and David Dodd. I got more interested in finding an investment analyst's job, listening to the managers and speaking to Murray.

In Train's *The New Money Masters*, I read that Jim Rogers,

a former partner of the billionaire investor George Soros, did not have an MBA. I read an article about Rogers' popular class on investment analysis at the Columbia Business School. I sat in his class for a semester, as one of many "non-paying students" as Rogers regularly reminded us. He asked the MBA students a series of questions about their research reports to buy or sell a stock.

One night, after Rogers finished his class, I left the building with him and asked how I could find a job as an investment analyst. He said to write brief research reports on companies and send them to fund managers. I asked if I should go to business school. He said invest $5,000 in stocks and, when I lost 80% of the money, I will have learned more about stock investing than from pursuing an MBA.

I read that Rogers liked electric utility stocks, due to rising long-term demand. Copying him, I made my first stock purchases in November 1989. I bought 50 shares of General Public Utilities, a company with good management and a high dividend yield, for about $45 each.

I also bought 300 shares of Pinnacle West Corp. for about $5 each. This Arizona utility's expansion into banking, real estate and a uranium venture caused several hundred million dollars in losses. The losses, some Wall Street analysts said, would bankrupt the company and wipe out shareholders.

Pinnacle's annual report showed its book value was $11 a share, more than twice my purchase price. I assumed this provided a margin of safety, the key to value investing, according to Benjamin Graham.

I also found that politicians rarely let utilities go bankrupt, fearing public criticism over the supervision by government agencies. A utility affects every voter, and each month they are reminded of the "good" or "bad" policies when they pay their bill.

A few weeks later, PacifiCorp, an Oregon utility, tried to buy Pinnacle for $8 in cash per share. That day Pinnacle's stock doubled and then kept rising as the bid was raised to $21, a few months later. I was lucky since I did not realize Pinnacle was understating its liabilities and hence its book value provided no margin of safety.

At *Forbes* I wrote stories on companies popular with value investors, like the check printer Deluxe which had consistent growth and rising profits. This business has shrunk due to the free electronic bill payments offered by banks.

I also wrote about insurance claims adjuster Crawford & Co., computer skills training company Programming & Systems and the Bible publisher Thomas Nelson.

Nelson's Chief Executive Sam Moore sent me a leather-bound Bible, with my name inscribed in gold letters after the story was published in August 1991. He had migrated to the U.S. from Lebanon in 1950, sponsored by a Baptist missionary. He supported himself at the University of South Carolina by selling Bibles from door to door.

Moore wrote a letter to Malcolm Forbes Jr, editor in chief, saying that I was not "willing to accept" any complimentary copies of books. I did not accept gifts and invitations to one-on-one meals from company and public relations executives. This was to keep an independent perspective, and since I did not want to answer their phone calls. But I kept the Bible that Moore sent after mentioning it to my editor.

The Bible, insurance claims adjustment and computer training business are still around. But many of the technology companies I wrote about, like Cabletron Systems, Vitalink and Novell, disappeared due to sudden shifts in demand and new rivals. This is a lesson I carried into my job of analyzing investments: companies in stable old economy businesses, while boring, often provide good long-term investments.

## Learning Financial Analysis

I followed Rogers' advice and mailed half page reports on a couple of stocks to fund managers while asking for a job. I picked stocks using ideas from fund reports and media interviews of successful managers. I based my analysis on insights from Lynch's books and Buffett's shareholder letters.

Boring companies in a boring business often make good investments, writes Peter Lynch in *One Up on Wall Street*. He had one of the best long term investment records as manager of Fidelity's flagship Magellan fund.

"Getting the story on a company is a lot easier if you understand the basic business. That's why I'd rather invest in panty hose than in communication satellites, or in motel chains than in fiber optics. The simpler it is, the better I like it. When somebody says, 'Any idiot could run this joint,' that's a plus as far as I'm concerned, because sooner or later any idiot probably is going to be running it," he says.

Buffett makes the same point saying that when a good manager runs a bad business, the reputation of the business remains intact.

When I come across a public company with cheap, valuable assets, in politically safe areas like the U.S., I am reminded of Lynch saying such assets cannot be easily replicated.

He also found "great investments in lousy industries" that have years of losses, lack of new investment and bankruptcy of weak competitors. This leads to sharp cuts in supply. So when demand picks up again the companies which survive enjoy pricing power and rising profits.

One good area to search for investments, Lynch says, is companies where executives buy stock by investing huge sums in relation to their salaries. He writes, "There's no better tip-off to the probable success of a stock than that people in the company are putting their own money into it. In general, corporate insiders are net sellers....After the 1,000-point drop from August to October, 1987, it was reassuring to discover that there were four shares bought to every one share sold by insiders across the board. At least they hadn't lost their faith."

I also follow Lynch's method of personally testing the attractiveness of a business, though not as rigorously. He stayed at La Quinta Inns, ate Dunkin Donuts and got haircuts at Supercuts.

Stocks I recommended for purchase included L.E.Myers, which provided construction services to electrical utilities; Columbia Hospital, a consolidator of for-profit hospitals; and Energy Services, now ENSCO International, which owns oil and gas drilling rigs.

I knew I was on the right path since several fund managers replied to my letters. George Michaelis of Source Capital said he would consider me when he had a job opening. A value investor profiled by John Train in "The New Money Masters", Michaelis died in an accident in 1996.

Another manager was Herb Ehlers of Eagle Asset Management and later at Goldman Sachs. He said the key factor he looked for in an analyst is interest.

I enrolled for the first level of the Chartered Financial Analyst's exam. This is a three-year rating system for finance professionals launched in 1959 and backed by Benjamin Graham. There were five areas covered in the exam, accounting, equity analysis, fixed income analysis, quantitative methods and ethics.

I joined a CFA study group, through the New York Society of Security Analysts. The group met at the midtown office of a Scandinavian bank, where Nicholas Mattachieri worked.

He and the eight others in the group were junior analysts at banks and brokerages. We focused on learning accounting during the weekly two-hour discussions. No one knew accounting and so the sessions were not very useful. But reading a chapter each week helped me prepare for the exam.

Some in the group took preparatory courses in New York, which charged $600 in fees. One group member attended a three-day weekend course held in Charlottesville, VA, where the CFA Institute is based.

The courses gave participants spiral bound notes of about 500 pages, summarizing the content of the textbooks. Each of the books for the five topics were several hundred pages thick.

Group members made copies for those who did not take the courses. I found the notes from the course at Charlottesville were clear and concise, a big help during my study for the exam.

The instructors were former officials of the institute, who had set questions and graded answers for the CFA exams. They used their inside knowledge to launch a more lucrative career, like many former members of Congress as well as senior officials in government, who work as lobbyists and advisers.

### Missing an Analyst's Job

I got more responses from fund managers after I passed the first CFA exam in June 1990. I wrote goaltender, college hockey team, on the last line of my one-page resume.

Was I crazy to be a goaltender, was the first question from the director of research of a major firm. A Boston native, he assumed I was an ice hockey goaltender, the key position in the team. I said I became a goaltender because it was the only way to get onto the team. I did not tell him that it was a field hockey team.

I met Fiona Biggs at Dreyfus; Carley Cunniff at Ruane Cunniff; Charles Kadlec and Paul Wick at J & W Seligman; Peter Kiely at Eaton Vance; Saul Pannell at Wellington; and Steve

Silverman, who managed the Merrill Lynch Pacific fund, through one of his analysts Stanley Brenner.

I met Jean-Marie Eveillard, manager of the $200 million SoGen (now First Eagle) Funds which consistently ranked on the Honor Roll in *Forbes'* annual mutual fund issue. He said he would consider me when the funds he managed grew larger and he was hiring more analysts.

He agreed to let me spend a couple of hours reading files on companies at his office. I wanted to see what data and information was used for analyzing an investment. A couple of value managers had declined my request. The SoGen files contained annual reports and other financial filings by a company, research reports from in-house and brokerage analysts and newspaper and magazine articles on the company and its executives.

I was very surprised to find Jean-Marie and other managers answering their phones. No editor took my calls when I was seeking a journalism job.

Peter Lynch and George Vanderheiden at Fidelity said they had passed on my stock research and resume to Rick Spillane, head of research. Fidelity was a top choice for an analyst since it had several good fund managers, and analysts got to manage sector funds after a couple of years. I went to Boston and met Spillane a couple of times.

Lynch retired from running the Magellan fund in 1990 but continued to advise analysts and managers at Fidelity. He manages investments for his foundation and other philanthropies.

In 2006, at an oil and gas investment conference in New York, I thanked him for taking my call when he was a big star. He asked what I was doing, about Christians in India and if the lack of manufacturing jobs made the poverty worse in India than in China. Manufacturing accounts for 17% of India's economy while it is 36% of China's.

I got to the final interviews at several fund companies but

did not have recommendations from fund managers and executives, needed to get most such jobs. An MBA would likely have helped me get such a recommendation from an adjunct teacher at a business school.

I also made errors. At one final round interview I asked the manager of a major fund if he was worried about the high valuations of stocks. This was in November 1990, when stock markets were falling - the S&P 500 Index fell 3.1% that year. It was a wrong question since the firm's managers focused on stock picking and not on trying to time the market.

Then, after a final round of interviews with three fund managers, the head of investments of a Boston firm called to ask when I could meet him. I said I would set up a meeting when I was next visiting the city. I should have said that I would see him the next day. I did not realize he probably wants to meet me to discuss a job offer.

## Picking Indian Stocks Which Were Losers

I nearly failed the second level CFA exam, once again due to problems with finishing essay-based exams. I had prepared well but was nervous since it was the toughest of the three exams. I studied late into the night and got no sleep.

I knew the answers to the questions for the morning exam, held at John Jay College. But I spent half the time answering a quarter of the questions. I thought of giving up on the exam, fearing I would fail. Instead I went to a restroom, washed my face, returned and answered as many questions as I could.

I also figured I could time my answers better during the afternoon exam. I jumped with joy when I opened the letter saying I had passed the exam, the only time I remember doing so in my adult years.

The CFA helped me find an analyst's job. I learned to analyze financial statements and got trained to read financial reports like 10-Ks filed by public companies by having to go through the dense data-filled textbooks for the CFA exams.

I continued mailing research reports to fund managers, roughly once a quarter, recommending purchase of stocks. I also asked if they had a job.

In October 1993, after I got my CFA, Jean-Marie asked me to meet his two analysts. SoGen Funds had grown to about $800 million. He hired me as an analyst and two years later gave me a small portfolio to manage.

Jean-Marie's outstanding record was based on value investing around the globe, buying cheap stocks of companies with good assets or strong businesses and which were typically not followed by major brokerage firms.

"Value investing is not an acquired taste. Either you like it immediately or you don't – either it's in your DNA or it's not...Knowledge of value investing does not promise automatic success. The willingness to swim upstream, patience, hard work, good luck and some skills – probably in that order – are also helpful, indeed necessary," he writes in his forthcoming book on global value investing.

He does not mind going against the crowd. "Warren Buffett said it takes temperament, not a high IQ, to be a successful long-term investor...you have to be willing to go against the grain – not systematically, because then you're simply a contrarian – but whenever you think it's appropriate," says Jean-Marie.

"Somebody once asked me, 'Well, how come?' I am not sure, but when I was growing up in France in the early 1950s, I went to Catholic Church on Sunday. The priest would get up for the sermon and say: 'Don't expect to be happy on this Earth; this is a valley of tears.' And so, contrary to many Americans who seem to expect to be happy every day, I'm more willing to face the suffering which is associated with swimming upstream... In life, most of what's worthwhile comes hard, whether it's playing baseball or investing in stocks."

He focused on identifying the key factors of a business and assessing a company's financial strength. He invested only after estimating that, in a worst case scenario, the stock price was unlikely to collapse causing a major and permanent loss.

His success was also based on what he did not own. He stayed away from overvalued Japanese stocks in the late 1980s and held no financial stocks before the 2008 stock market collapse.

"I usually stayed away from stocks of financial institutions...Banks became quasi-hedge funds...They took on huge leverage, with debt to equity ratios of up to 30 to 1 or more...If assets go down 4%, you are – at least temporarily—insolvent...Today, I'm not sure what banking is and will be like. As Paul Volcker put it: the only good financial innovation was the ATM," Jean-Marie writes.

He gave his analysts the freedom to search for investing opportunities in a wide range of industries, though avoiding high technology businesses since they change rapidly and are not easy to understand and analyze.

At times, based on his reading, he would ask an analyst to research a company or industry. He did not micromanage and dictate what to do. He did not criticize or shout at his analysts and employees, unlike some well-known fund managers. He showed he liked an analyst's work by buying or selling a stock, based on an analyst's recommendation.

My stock picks at SoGen, which performed well, included Scandinavian Broadcasting, which owned commercial television stations competing against state broadcasters; uniform rental company Unifirst; and Fast Retailing, the parent of the Japanese chain Uniqlo. The retailer, which started by selling discount clothing to the Japanese during the 1990's recession, is a global store brand known for good designs, quality and attractive prices.

My stock selections that suffered losses embarrassingly included two related to India - a closed end India fund listed in Dublin and Gujarat State Fertilizers. Fortunately Jean-Marie invested very little in these stocks.

Jean-Marie is humble, admits when he does not know something and warns against trying to be too smart or cute while investing. He was a fair and generous employer and a very rare Wall Street boss, with an unconventional outlook.

## Chapter 14

## FUNDING FREE CLASSIC BOOKS

I set up Banyan Tree Capital Management in 2000, eager to start my own fund. Looking back, this was a dumb move. I may have had the intellectual skills, but I knew few wealthy people and had no contacts at institutions who could invest in my fund. Also, unlike me, most managers who succeed with their own funds in the U.S. went to business schools and worked for several years at major Wall Street firms.

Most important, in addition to a good pedigree, they start out with a team of professionals. They get initial financial backing and investment from former colleagues at Wall Street firms, college and business school friends and from funds that seed new funds.

Even so, many of them take five, seven or more years to become financially viable. I started Banyan on my own, without a team of analysts, operations and marketing partners and, having worked at SoGen for only about six years, with very little savings.

The thesis for my fund was that the Internet bubble of the late 1990s would burst and cheap value stocks would show superior performance. Banyan was up in the high teens from July 2000 to March 2002 while the S&P 500 was down 17%.

This performance attracted attention from major investors, some of whom I admired for both their investment success and philanthropy. They, however, lost interest since I did not have a team and managed a very small fund. I later found out that both these obstacles could have been easily tackled by teaming up with a larger investment group.

Then the fund started performing badly as the stock market continued falling, and that too sharply, from April to July 2002. This was after news of the accounting scandals at Enron and WorldCom surfaced.

Cheap good stocks, like those owned by Banyan, had big declines during those four months. I had used some leverage to buy more stocks in March and this too hurt the fund. Some clients pulled their money and stocks were sold near the bottom of the market. These stocks recovered strongly after August but it did not help Banyan's performance in 2002.

I decided to never use leverage again. To understand the causes for my error, I read books on fund managers who made major errors and how they recovered. I found that many successful investors had faced similar personal obstacles: guilt over money.

Growing up in India, there were only a handful of role models of good business owners, like the Tata's, who were said to follow ethical practices. Up until the 1980s when the information technology business took off, there were few opportunities to launch a business based on intellectual content. Starting even an education or publishing business, for instance, required paying bribes to politicians and bureaucrats for the licenses.

The business experience of relatives and friends was also discouraging. My older brother George did all the work to set up an ice cream retail business and a yard for building boats. He got no financial rewards from the owners who funded the business.

Unlike others on Wall Street, I had no dreams of becoming rich and being able to buy luxury homes, airplanes and fancy cars.

I wanted to do work I enjoyed, be independent and, as George Harrison put it, have enough money to be free to do what I wanted - not having to worry about being fired.

I decided to continue managing funds since my stock selections were fine and I enjoy the work. I also plan to give any money I make to expanding access to education and civil liberties. I care about these issues due to my experiences.

Banyan performed well during the severe stock market decline in 2008 and 2009. I did not make full use of rare investment opportunities, including finding stocks selling below the net cash on the balance sheet. Perhaps I was scarred by the 2002 experience.

In education, an initial goal is to translate a hundred major classics in literature, science, history, philosophy, astronomy and other subjects, which are the pillars of modern rational thought, into the twenty two major Indian languages. These translations, as well as Spanish editions in the U.S., will be distributed free online and as print copies to schools and libraries.

In the area of civil liberties, one goal is to provide online tools to publish and distribute reports that expose human rights abuse in various parts of the world.

My journey continues to fund the attainment of these goals.

# Appendix A

## *THE ECONOMIST* THRIVES

I was a regular reader of *The Economist* since age 18, spending over an hour on its concise insights into key global political, economic, business and finance issues as well as on arts, science and technology. The weekly magazine was founded in 1843 by a Scottish hat maker to champion free trade, internationalism and minimum interference by governments, especially in the affairs of the market.

I continue to read *The Economist*, especially its coverage of arts, science and technology, though occasionally since I read several newspapers each day. I also read it when I want a quick summary of a major current issue.

For instance, to understand the implications of Scotland's 2014 referendum for independence, I read the articles on the topic in the magazine's July edition that year. "The campaign has been a bad-tempered one, marked by growing Scottish anger at English complacency and indifference while the English resentment of Scottish whingeing and freeloading has risen; only a strong vote for the (British) union will bury this issue," the editorial noted in typical opinionated style.

*The Economist* (and *The Financial Times*) continue to prosper amid competition from free online sources over the past two decades. In contrast *The New York Times, The Wall Street Journal, The Washington Post, Time* and *Newsweek,* all with affluent readers, have seen sharp declines in circulation and advertising revenues and sharply reduced profits and, in some cases, losses.

The decline began in the mid-1990s when these and other legacy print publishers allowed free online access to their stories and photographs via AOL, Yahoo and Google. They also allowed their content, created through costly reporting and editorial work, to be re-packaged and distributed for free by new online competitors known as aggregators.

Many print readers cancelled their subscriptions of the legacy publications since the stories were available free online. These publications, seeking to stem revenue declines, began restricting access to their online content and charging a subscription fee. *The New York Times* began charging for online content in March 2011.

But most of the potential younger audience for legacy print publishers get their news from *Business Insider, BuzzFeed, The Huffington Post, Vice* and other free online sites. They do not want to pay subscription fees to access the information.

The free online publishers carry brief stories, mostly based on content from other sources, top ten lists, celebrity gossip, quizzes and lots of photos and cat videos. Their goal is to grow their audience and lift advertising revenues.

One of their recent revenue strategies, which some legacy publishers have also adopted, is native advertising. This is content created by the editorial staff for advertisers. It is placed amid editorial content thereby blurring the line which separates editorial and advertising information.

Free online publishers are attracting hundreds of millions of dollars from eager investors, including major venture capital firms as well as traditional media businesses like Hearst Corp and

Rupert Murdoch's 21st Century Fox.

The German media company Axel Springer bought 97% of *Business Insider* in 2015 for about $450 million, while Amazon founder Jeff Bezos owns the rest. Such funding is enabling the free online publishers to hire more journalists to rewrite stories from other sources and to create original content.

*The Economist* is in a strong position since it followed a different strategy from that of its legacy print rivals. It did not give free online access to its content and its website offers non-subscribers only brief teasers for some older stories. The content, largely analysis based on facts and data, is also difficult for the online aggregators to summarize and convert into popular stories on their free websites.

The magazine continues to be a weekly must read for a growing English educated global audience ranging from academics, like students at the Centre for Development Studies in India where I got my M.Phil., to professionals on Wall Street.

Its circulation has grown consistently reaching 1.6 million in 2015, up from one million in 2006. Three quarters of new and renewing subscribers pay for digital and print subscriptions and it has over 100,000 digital only subscribers.

*The Economist* does not offer discount subscriptions via Amazon or Groupon. During the November 2015 Black Friday sales on Amazon, for instance, U.S. annual subscriptions were slashed 90% for *Bloomberg Businessweek*, from $300 to $25, and the bi-weekly *Fortune*, from $116 to $12.

*The Economist* was sold at its full price, $127 for annual digital access and $160 for digital and print formats in the U.S. The subscription fees provide *The Economist* with a stable, recurring source of revenue.

Its affluent global audience, reached via high priced, undiscounted digital and print subscriptions, is very attractive to advertisers selling global brands like watches, alcohol, apparel and luxury cars. Several publications, ranging from *The New York Times* to new digital ones like the *Quartz,* are trying to replicate the editorial and business strategies of *The Economist.*

In 2014 Bloomberg hired the editor of *The Economist,* John Micklethwait, as editor in chief of *Bloomberg News.* Bloomberg owns platforms in various media including TV, radio and in print, *Bloomberg Businessweek.*

The strength of *The Economist's* strategy became evident in August 2015 when the London based Pearson PLC sold its 50% non-controlling stake in The Economist Group to other shareholders, including magazine employees. This cash transaction valued the business at about $1.5 billion. For the year ended March 31, 2015, The Economist Group had $94 million in operating profit on $521 million in revenues.

Earlier in July 2015, Pearson also sold The Financial Times Group to Japan's leading business media group Nikkei Inc. for $1.3 billion. In contrast Amazon founder Jeff Bezos paid only $250 million to buy *The Washington Post* in August 2013.

Like *The Economist, The Financial Times* does not provide free access to its online content. Three quarters of its 720,000 daily global circulation comes from digital subscribers and a year's subscription is about $700, accounting for much of its revenues. Nikkei's purchase, following an intense bidding war, was at a steep price of about $1,800 per subscriber. The Financial Times Group's 2015 revenues were $512 million and profit $37 million.

Exor increased its stake in The Economist Group to 43% in the 2015 transaction. It is a fund run by Italy's Agnelli family.

John Elkann, 39-year-old chairman of Exor, has been a regular reader of the weekly magazine since he was a teenager. He justified the high purchase price for the partial ownership telling William Cohan, for a story in *The New York Times* on November 23, 2015, "If you have a distinct journalistic offer, which is independent; if you have a readership, which is growing in the world.... and if you have the technology that can help you reach them.... the combination of that...is pretty powerful."

The unique value of *The Economist,* which numerous web-based rivals are yet to disrupt, is summed up by Eric Schmidt, Executive Chairman of Google. The magazine's website carries this quote from him: "Life without *The Economist* would be life without a global perspective."

## Appendix B

# DISRUPTING FOR-PROFIT

# ACADEMIC PUBLISHING

*The Journal of Peasant Studies* published my review of B.S. Baviskar's "The Politics of Development: Sugar Co-operatives in Rural Maharashtra" in October 1982. I had written it a year earlier, during my first semester for an M.Phil. at the Center for Development Studies in India. The book by the sociologist did not discuss the economic and political power of the farmers who control the cooperatives.

Like the other authors, I was not paid a fee for the article, but I did not care since it was an academic honor. I realized that I could get research papers published in reputed journals, a major help if I were to pursue an academic career. The journal, being well designed and printed on quality paper, gave a feeling of having achieved something permanent.

Later, while working as an investment analyst in New York, I was not surprised to find that for-profit academic publishers are very profitable businesses. On the cost side they typically do not pay authors for creating the products they sell, and on the revenue side they charge very high prices to subscribers, which are mostly not-for-profit libraries.

Studies show that libraries pay four to ten times more per page for journals from for-profit publishers compared to what they pay to subscribe to journals from non-profit publishers like academic associations. Also, the for-profit journals typically raise prices every year since they have little competition.

In the case of textbooks, prices in the U.S. have risen at three times the rate of inflation since the 1980s, according to a 2014 story in *The Economist*.

*The Journal of Peasant Studies* is published by Taylor & Francis, whose origins date back to 1798 when Richard Taylor published the first edition of *The Philosophical Magazine*, a pioneering scientific journal from an independent company.

Today, Taylor & Francis publishes over 1,800 academic journals and some 2,000 books a year and has a catalog of over 55,000 books. Its strategy in the journal business is to drive "higher value subscriptions."

In 2015 the price of an online-only annual subscription for six issues of *The Journal of Peasant Studies* was $845 for an educational institution in the U.S. and $966 for both print and online issues.

Taylor is part of U.K. based Informa PLC. It is a public company that operates in three businesses: academic publishing, business data and conferences.

Academic publishing is the largest division. In 2015, it accounted for nearly 40% of Informa's sales of $1,758 million. The business had an operating profit margin of 37%.

Such attractive business economics have made for-profit academic publishers great investments since the 1980s. Investors include private equity firms who buy such companies by investing small amounts of equity since the free cash flow from the business supports a huge debt load.

I did not get an author's fee when the Oxford University Press (OUP) published my essay on Indian entrepreneurs in the

U.S. in the 2007, 2011 and 2012 editions of a book. The 2012 edition of *The New Oxford Companion to Economics in India* sells at a list price of $275. (An essay on Indian Entrepreneurs in the U.S. is in Appendix C.)

OUP is the world's largest university publisher, printing 300 journals and thousands of books each year. Both revenue and profit margins at OUP keep growing. In the year ended March 2015 the publisher had an after-tax profit of $143 million on revenue of $1,180 million.

OUP is a department of Oxford University and so uses its profits to serve educational goals. In fiscal 2015, OUP gave $260 million to Oxford University to fund research, scholarships and other activities. It also provides some free access to online journals as well as cheaper access to journals, scholarly online services and medical books to education institutions in developing countries.

One can debate the ethics of for-profit academic publishers enjoying monopoly profits using free labor and selling high priced goods to universities, libraries and other non-profit institutions.

But their continued business success is an anomaly when profits of most traditional print publishers like newspapers and magazines have been slashed over the past two decades by new online rivals, many of whom like *The Huffington Post* also do not pay most of their contributors.

A few new non-profit publications are generating much goodwill among librarians and academics who are seeking to help curtail rising education costs.

In 2004, the editorial board of *The Journal of Algorithms*, published by for-profit Elsevier, resigned protesting the near doubling in the journal's price per page over the years 1997 to 2002. The revolt was led by Donald Knuth, a founding editor of the journal and a professor at Stanford University's department of computer science.

His book *The Art of Computer Programing* is considered a

classic in scientific texts. Knuth and the editorial board began publishing a non-profit journal *ACM Transactions on Algorithms* with the Association for Computing Machinery, distributed free to the association's members. In 2010, Elsevier, part of the RELX Group, stopped publishing its journal.

A more recent example is *The Journal of the Association of Environmental and Resource Economists*. It is published by the University of Chicago press since 2014. Members of the association get free online access to the journal. The annual membership fee for joining the group is $62.

A library in a medium-sized academic institution pays $430 for an annual online subscription and $495 for print and online, with the maximum rate for a large university being $574.

The association's journal competes with *The Journal of Environmental Economics and Management* published by Elsevier. Its list price for an annual subscription is $1,780 for an academic library in the U.S. and also in India, and rises to $1,902 for libraries in institutions which have over 50,000 full-time students, faculty and researchers.

Few non-profit academic journals are being published, despite interest from academics and the cost savings to libraries and educational institutions. A major reason is the time and effort academics must volunteer to publish a peer reviewed journal to displace a long established for-profit journal. For instance, it took the Association of Environmental Economists ten years to launch their journal.

But another traditional publishing business is ripe for disruption, by non-profit entrepreneurs teaming up with academic associations and university publishers. They can together use the low cost and relative ease of online publishing and enable more academic associations to publish low price journals and books.

# Appendix C

# INDIAN ENTREPRENEURS IN THE U.S.

Since the 1980s, several thousand professionals of Indian origin have set up technology enterprises in the U.S. Businesses founded or co-founded by them include Cascade Communications, Daisy Systems, Epitome, Hotmail, Junglee, Morphotek, Solar Junction and TIBCO Software.

Several Indian entrepreneurs have become major venture capitalists. They include Promod Haque, an electrical engineer from Delhi University and an MBA from Northwestern University's Kellogg School of Management. He has invested in more than seventy companies and has created over $40 billion in exit values, by companies going public or being acquired, since joining Norwest Venture Partners in 1990.

Naval Ravikant is a venture capitalist riding the recent social networking wave. He grew up with little money in Delhi and New York and washed dishes to fund himself through Dartmouth College. He helped found successful websites epinions.com and vast.com and was an early investor in major successful start-ups Uber, Twitter and Foursquare.

In 2009, Ravikant co-founded AngelList. In 2015 it enabled 441 start-ups to raise $163 million from about 3,400 investors, including major venture capital firms. "I'm always rooting for the small guy...call it growing up as a poor, fat, immigrant kid," he told *The New York Times*, March 7, 2011.

A striking aspect about professionals turned entrepreneurs in the U.S. is that many of them are not from business families and castes. Their advanced skills and habits of hard work, coupled with a perceptive grasp of potential demand for a product or service, give them a major edge in setting up a business which is based on intellectual content.

A good example is Vinod Khosla, an electrical engineer from the Indian Institute of Technology, Delhi, with a Masters' in biomedical engineering from Carnegie Mellon University and an MBA from Stanford University.

He was a co-founder of Sun Microsystems. He then joined the venture capital firm Kleiner Perkins Caufield & Byers where his successes include Cerent, which was sold to Cisco Systems for $7 billion, and failures include Dynabook. He grew up "in an Indian army household with no business or technology connections," according to his biography, on the website of Khosla Ventures, which he founded.

Like all entrepreneurs, the Indians in the U.S. are motivated by a business challenge and also want to become rich. They realize that job security, as in a job for life, does not exist in the U.S.

Also, in case a start-up fails, as nine out of ten do, they know that they will likely find another high-paying job. The business culture accepts failure and application of lessons learned to another business or job. So professionals are willing to take the leap from well-paying jobs into the risk of starting an enterprise

Capital raising and successful exits are also far easier in the U.S. Often the initial capital required to set enterprises based on intellectual content is small, in some cases a few thousand dollars.

The initial funding comes from friends, family and angel investors. The investors and entrepreneurs hope to make good gains, if the business shows signs of success, by selling the company or through a stock market listing.

There are also several firms started by Indians in the U.S., which secure contracts reserved for racial minorities and women by government agencies and semi-government operations, like city transportation and airports, and regulated businesses like power, telephone and financial services.

These Indians claim they suffer handicaps similar to African Americans, Hispanics and American Indians. But they try to avoid publicity over their minority-owned business status since they are upper caste Indians educated at good universities.

In India, several factors have made it more conducive for professionals to start an enterprise. The post-1991 growth in the Indian economy has boosted all business. Also, in the late 1990s, demand for Indian IT services surged due to fears that computer systems worldwide would freeze on January 1, 2000, the Y2K issue.

Then, after the Internet bubble collapsed in 2000, IT jobs were slashed in the U.S., and there was another wave of work outsourced to India.

Successful professionals turned entrepreneurs in India include the seven engineers who founded Infosys in 1981 with $250 in capital. The global IT services company has a market capitalization of $37 billion, making N.R. Narayana Murthy and the other founders celebrated billionaires.

Another example is Biocon founded in 1978 by Kiran Mazumdar-Shaw with $1,000 to export a plant enzyme used by the brewing industry. Biocon, based in Bangalore, had sales of about $500 million in 2015.

The opportunity for professionals to start businesses is very large in India. In addition to information technology, professionals have a major advantage in areas like web based information, retailing, financial and other services, education, engineering and medical research and services, media, publishing, equity brokerage and money management.

Since 2010, these areas have attracted investments from major foreign venture and private equity funds and businesses, including Sequoia Capital, Warburg Pincus and Tiger Global from the U.S. and China's online giant Alibaba.

Over $5 billion was invested by these and other funds into new ventures in India in 2015, ten times greater than in 2010. There were about 4,200 start-ups in India in 2015, triple the number that were operating five years earlier.

The flow of foreign money has opened up access to capital for professionals in India to start ventures, especially services based on mobile phones which are more widely used than other internet devices in India. Eight Indian enterprises, funded by foreign investors, have valuations of over $1 billion, including online retailer Snapdeal, mobile payment system Paytm and online retailer Flipkart, which has the biggest valuation at $15 billion.

Indian parents are now more accepting of children giving up stable, professional jobs to start their own business, because of the major success of some entrepreneurs since 2010, Bhavish Aggarwal told James Crabtree of *The Financial Times* in 2016.

Aggarwal is the founder of the taxi app Ola, which raised $1.2 billion from Japan's Softbank, a Chinese partner and other investors and is valued at $5 billion. He is a graduate of the Indian Institute of Technology, Mumbai. His father, a doctor, did not speak to him for six months after he gave up a job with Microsoft in Bangalore to start a business, which grew into Ola.

Some professionals turned entrepreneurs in India are funding major philanthropic efforts. One of them is Aziz Premji, an electrical engineer from Stanford and founder of the IT Company Wipro, with a market value of $27 billion. He is pursuing long term solutions to improve the availability of good public education, from early schooling to graduate levels. So the spread of entrepreneurship, while not a cure for India's poverty, illiteracy and malnutrition, will be a force for positive change.

# ACKNOWLEDGMENTS

I have mentioned many of those who helped me through my six degrees in this book.

In addition, I am grateful to:

In the U.S.- Barry Abramson, Sima Ariam, Brook Boyd, Thomas Brady, Thomas Cea, Marcia Chithelen, David Cheung, Daria Deshuk, Nina Frantzen, Marc Gabelli, Carol Huston, Donna R. Leatherman, Norman Morales, Salvatore Muoio, Regina Niro, Rodrigo Roman, Stimson Schantz, Peter Slatin, Jesse and Brooke Stuart, Anne Weitzer, Audrey Wennblom, Marian Williams, Doug Wilson, Mohammed Zafar and the staff at the Columbia and Princeton Club of New York, where I did the writing on weekends.

In India- A. J. C. Bose, Mahesh Hira, Thapan Mukherjee, Hrushikesh Panda, S. Ramanathan, Vijay Raut, Dilip Suryavanshi, Badruddin Topiwalla and my brother Joseph and sister Theresa.

For the writing and production- Lisa Shuchter, Annette Kondo and Gary Shapiro for editorial help; Rajaram Dasgupta for refocusing the book; Andy Lee for his criticisms; Harish Bhonsle, Dirk McDonnell, Thomas Vinciguerra and D. Kelly Jones for comments on parts of the book; Visakh Menon for designing the cover; Natalie Chithelen for design suggestions; also Julio Pereryra; Spencer Cheng at Bryant Park Publishers, which I co-founded and advice, for handling the technical issues.

www.ingramcontent.com/pod-product-compliance
Lightning Source LLC
Chambersburg PA
CBHW020613300426
44113CB00007B/627